Preface

Students across the nation have been using the Speaking Solutions Nifty 50-59 Training Manuals to learn speech and handwriting recognition skills since 2002. We are proud to introduce our newest speech recognition training manual "Speech Recognition Applications: The Basics and Beyond."

Speech recognition technology has made numerous advancements over the past decade and has become easier to use and much more efficient. Speech recognition software is now being used by more and more individuals in a wide variety of industries and professional careers every day. Most people can create documents using speech recognition software much faster than they can type. By learning to use speech as an alternate input method, students and professionals will increase their overall productivity and acquire a valuable skill that will give them a competitive edge as they advance in their education and careers.

About this Book

Speech Recognition Applications: The Basics and Beyond provides step-by-step directions for getting started with speech recognition software. It also provides instruction in developing the basic speech recognition skills needed to dictate, correct, edit and format a variety of documents. Exercises are included for creating letters, reports and macros along with navigating the Internet by voice and creating e-mails.

This book focuses on Dragon Dictate® for the MAC which is currently the only speech recognition software available for the Mac Platform as of 2011. The unique design of this book offers a perfect training solution for students, teachers, and business professionals. It offers easy to follow lessons with step-by-step directions and many screen shots and tips. The exercises will help you learn how to use speech recognition as a daily input device and will help you improve your overall speed and accuracy.

Learning outcomes

When you have completed this book, you will be able to demonstrate mastery of speech recognition skills, which includes:
- creating and managing a speech profile
- properly using microphone
- using correct commands
- navigating, formatting, correcting, editing, saving and printing by voice
- dictating at over 100 words a minute at 98% accuracy or above
- preparing correctly formatted documents including e-mail messages, letters, reports, tables and spreadsheets

TABLE OF CONTENTS

LESSON 5--Selecting and Dictating

LESSON 6--Correcting

LESSON 7--Reinforcing Dictation Skills & Evaluating Progress

LESSON 8--Enhancing Your Speech Profile

LESSON 9--Using Commands

LESSON 10--Dictation, Correction & Formatting Concepts

LESSON 11--Web Navigation, E-Mails and Help

LESSON 12--Reinforcement Activities

INTRODUCTION—Learning About Speech Recognition

Speech recognition is one of the most sophisticated technologies ever created for the personal computer. Speech recognition products use the human voice as the main interface between the user and the computer. Speaker–dependent speech recognition systems, such as Dragon NaturallySpeaking and DragonDictate® from Nuance Communications, create an individual voice profile for each user of the system. The voice profile contains information about the unique characteristics of each person's voice along with a customized set of words, known as a vocabulary, and user-specific information including software settings and personalized voice commands.

Speech Recognition Background

Research into this area spans over five decades. The earliest attempts to devise systems for automatic speech recognition were made in the 1950s. Much of the early research leading to the development of speech activation and recognition technology was funded by NSA, NSF and the Defense Department's DARPA in the 1980s.

In 1985, Raymond "Ray" Kurzweil, an American inventor and futurist, introduced the Kurzweil Voice System, the first 1,000-word discrete-speech recognizer. This interface, adaptable to many applications, allowed the user to control the application by voice without modifying the operating system or software. In 1987, Kurzweil introduced the first 20,000-word discrete-speech recognizer, which was incorporated into Kurzweil Voice Report software and allowed users to create structured reports by voice. This speech recognition technology was designed initially for individuals in the disability community.

The early versions of speech recognition products were clunky and hard to use. The early language-recognition systems had to make compromises: they were "tuned" to be dependent on a particular speaker, or had small vocabulary, or used a very stylized and rigid syntax.

In 1994, Kurzweil successfully developed fully operational continuous dictation. This led to the development of continued speech recognition (CSR). Kurzweil Educational Systems is still well-known today for developing products to assist people with learning difficulties, and those who are blind or visually impaired, but other companies have become more involved with developing and improving speech software.[1]

The continuous speech recognition system became available in the first Dragon product in April of 1997. Of open Excel open Excel The computers required to run CSR easily cost $3500 at that time and were very primitive by today's standards. A large barrier to effective use of speech recognition was the lack of speed and accuracy due to low processing speeds and lack of RAM. This barrier, in addition to the high cost of hardware and inadequate headsets, made every day use of speech recognition a challenge.

---

[1]Intelligence, Automatic Speech Recognition (ASR) Speech / Voice Recognition, http://www.globalsecurity.org/intell/systems/asr.htm, Accessed September 20, 2010.

Improvements

The development of modern, high-speed PC processors in 2002 helped improve the speed and accuracy of speech recognition software. Both computer hardware and speech recognition software programs have had significant improvements over the past few years. Today, the average CPU is 1 GHz and has RAM levels of at least 1 GB making computers much more efficient. Many time-savings features have also been added to the software versions.

Originally, before the user could start dictating, they had to "train" the software by reading a series of passages that took about 45 minutes. Even after completing this initial training, the early versions were only about 75% accurate to begin with. Today, training the computer by reading passages takes less than 5 minutes and is optional. The out-of-the-box accuracy is about 95%.[2]

The average user can speak three times faster than they can type and can achieve remarkable accuracy at dictation speeds well over 100 words per minute with little effort. However, it does take time and patience at first to learn how to voice-write, edit, and format documents. The time and effort you will spend in learning how to use speech recognition software effectively will save you a tremendous amount of time in the future and will increase your overall productivity. Think of all the things that you may compose on a daily basis: emails, reports, databases, spreadsheet data, press releases, minutes, articles, newsletters, books, dissertations, white papers, journals— you name it. Consider how much time you will save if you can produce these documents three times faster using voice-input instead of the keyboard.

Techno-journalist David Pogue had this to say about learning to use speech recognition software:

> *"But most people, alas, simply don't have the **patience**. There are so many times in life when an investment in time and learning up front leads to a long-term payoff. And in computing, that's especially true (learning to use macros in Word, learning a few keyboard shortcuts in Mac OS X, and so on). Dictation software falls squarely in that category. "For me, it's a lifesaver and very nearly magical — but only because **I stuck with it.** "*[3]

Learning a New Skill

Over the past several years, the expanded use of cell phones, mobile devices and the Internet has transformed us into a very text intensive society. Dictating, composing, and reading out loud are awkward for many people at first. Dictating or "voicing our thoughts" to a computer is different than writing or keying our thoughts. Before word processors were popular, most people would write everything on paper before they keyed it into the computer even when they could type faster than they could write. Now most people are comfortable in keying their thoughts directly into the computer without writing anything down first. It took time and practice to change our thought process and habits from "thinking and writing" to "thinking and keying/texting."It will also take time and practice to change our thought process from "thinking and keying/texting" to "thinking and dictating."

---

[2]Wood, Lamont, 15 July 2007 Special to LiveScience , "Speech Recognition Software Finally Works" http://www.livescience.com/technology/070716_speech_recognition.html, Accessed September 20, 2010
3(David Pogue, FROM THE DESK OF DAVIED POGUE: Learning to Talk to Your PC, New York Times, March 2004).

Current Uses for Speech Recognition

Speech recognition technology has advanced to the point where it is being used by more and more individuals in a wide variety of industries and professional careers every day. Most people can create documents using speech recognition software much faster than they can type. By learning to use speech as an alternate input method, students and professionals will increase their overall productivity and acquire a valuable skill that will give them a competitive edge as they advance in their education and careers. Because speech recognition software is being utilized by leading corporate, government, legal, criminal justice, education and medical organizations throughout the world, learning to use speech recognition effectively could increase employment opportunities.

Industries Currently Using Speech Recognition Technology

Healthcare

Dragon NaturallySpeaking is the most widely used speech recognition application in healthcare industry and is being used by a wide variety of healthcare workers including doctors, medical students, nurses, physician assistants, nurse practitioners, dentists, physical/occupational therapists, pharmacists, administrators, medical assistants, and other support staff. Hospitals rely on the technology to improve financial performance and raise the quality of care because physicians are able to dictate more detailed notes, in real time into the patient records system. This allows quicker access to the information by other clinicians and healthcare workers who provide the patient with care.

Currently, 21st Century technology offers physicians and health care providers a medical record paradigm that will not only vastly upgrade the process of producing, maintaining and safeguarding medical records but will, in a direct and fundamental way, actually improve the quality of medical care. The technology is Electronic Medical Records (EMRs).[3] The $19 billion dollars provided in the Federal Stimulus Bill has given a large incentive for health care to implement an EMR system and requires all medical facilities to upgrade to an EMR system by 2012. EMRs produce the most accurate and complete patient health record possible to date and help physicians share information and practice better medicine.

Although most of the current high-end Electronic Medical Record products have 'pick lists' or 'click and point' methodology to complete large portions of the patient medical record, the historical portion of the patient medical record typically has a great deal of information that cannot be easily foreseen by the developers and is text intensive. Therefore, speech input is more productive.

3Fisherman, Eric, Voice Recognition, 2005
http://www.voicerecognition.com/electronicmedicalrecord/emrvoice/Accessed September 20, 2010.

Legal

Thousands of legal professionals incorporate speech recognition technology to dramatically reduce the time it takes to create everything from briefs and contracts to case documentation and correspondence. Law firms and legal departments deploy speech solutions broadly to speed document turnaround, reduce transcription costs, and streamline repetitive workflows – without having to change business processes or existing information systems. Each organization and even the individuals within each organization, use speech recognition for different purposes, based on their responsibilities, workflow, preferences, and other applications used. Speech recognition users include partners, associates, corporate counsel, judges, legal researchers, court reporters, law students, paralegals, mobile professionals, people with disabilities, transcriptionists, assistants, and other support staff.

Law Enforcement

Police departments use speech recognition to voice-enable patrol car computers to speed up the information collection and inquiry processes. Officers can dictate information an average of 68% faster than typing by hand. This enables the quick and safe completion of necessary paperwork and computer related tasks while on duty – providing additional time to focus on more important aspects of law enforcement, such as suppressing crime and patrolling the streets. It is used from uniformed patrol officers to the undercover vice detectives; from robbery/homicide investigators to school resource officers; from police service technicians to dispatchers and civilian support personnel.

Insurance

In today's insurance organizations, data entry often consumes the majority of a customer service representative's or agent's workday, limiting the amount of time they spend working on obtaining new clients for an agency. Using the keyboard to create reports and documentation is time-consuming, and organizations are plagued by high error rates, inconsistencies and slower processes. Speech recognition allows agents to document claims faster, more accurately and in a much more cost-effective manner. This allows the company to better manage heavy workloads, reduce overhead and provide better customer service.

Other Professions

Speech recognition is being used by many reporters, newspaper columnists, magazine editors, and authors. Careers such as closed caption, CART reporters for hearing-impaired individuals, and Internet streaming text providers, are also becoming more popular for voice inputting. The use of speech recognition technology will continue to increase as more and more industries learn the benefits and cost-effectiveness of this emerging inputting device.

Introducing speech recognition to students early in their academic development increases their ability to succeed during their secondary and post-secondary education, and it provides them with a valuable skill for future employment.

LESSON 1—Getting Started

Before you can use speech recognition software effectively, you must create a user profile and adjust your microphone. Multiple users can be set up on the same computer system. When you add a user, a separate profile or folder is created that stores the individual user's unique voice files. This profile stores acoustic information about your voice that the software uses to recognize what you say and updates your own individual speech vocabulary as you add or customize, specialized words, names, acronyms, and abbreviations--thus, improving accuracy each time you use your voice profile. (If the Dragon Dictate software is not installed on your computer, see software installation guide)

1.1—Create Profile

Dragon Dictate

Start Dragon Dictate by choosing Go, Applications and Click the **Dragon** icon

The first time you use Dragon Dictate, you will be prompted to create a new profile. The Profile Creation dialog box should open automatically. If it doesn't, you can choose **Tools, Profile** on the Dictate toolbar.

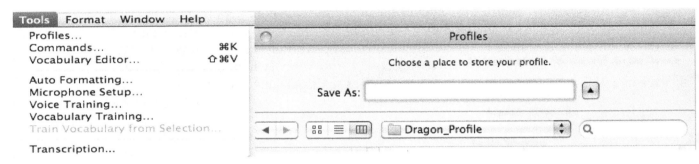

Most users want to set up their profile to save in a specific location such as a particular folder, network location or removable jump drive. You need to do this when first creating your profile by choosing the place to store your profile. (The sample below shows the profile being stored on a flash drive, inside a folder called Dragon Profile. However, if you are using your own personal computer you may just want to create a folder on your hard drive or desktop).

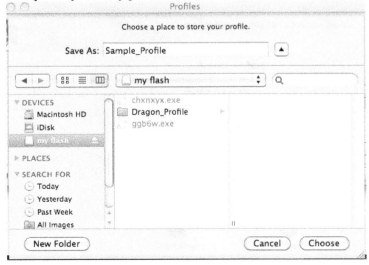

Create your own profile by choosing the storage location and keying in your name.

Now you can follow the step-by-step wizard directions for creating a profile:

Be sure your **USB microphone** headset is plugged in and choose the USB Audio Device from microphone drop down arrow if it is not already selected.

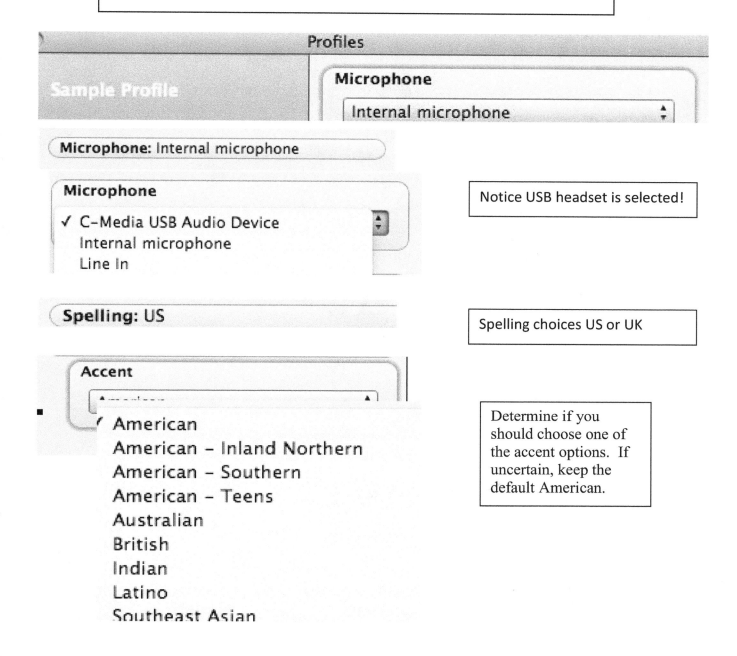

Click continue—the following screen will appear showing the proper position of your microphone.

Connecting a Microphone to your Macintosh

A Nuance-approved microphone for Mac is required in order to achieve the best accuracy and receive technical support.

If your microphone has analog connectors, plug them into the appropriate receptacles in a USB audio adapter and then plug the adapter into an open USB port on your computer.

Positioning Headset Microphones

Do not place the microphone directly in front of your mouth. Place it off to the side, about a thumb's width away from the corner of your mouth. Make sure the correct side, the side with the word "talk" or a dot, is facing you.

Other Microphones

Refer to your microphone's user manual for important information on setup and use.

Note: Microphone quality and positioning significantly affect recognition accuracy.

☐ Don't show this information again.   (OK)

Click OK –this screen will appear indicating your profile is being created.

Dragon Dictate

Making Profile "Sample Profile"...

Dragon Dictate

Loading Selection Grammar...

1.2 Check Microphone

Once your profile has been created, you will need to complete the steps for setting up your microphone. (You will also check your microphone on a daily basis by following these steps.)

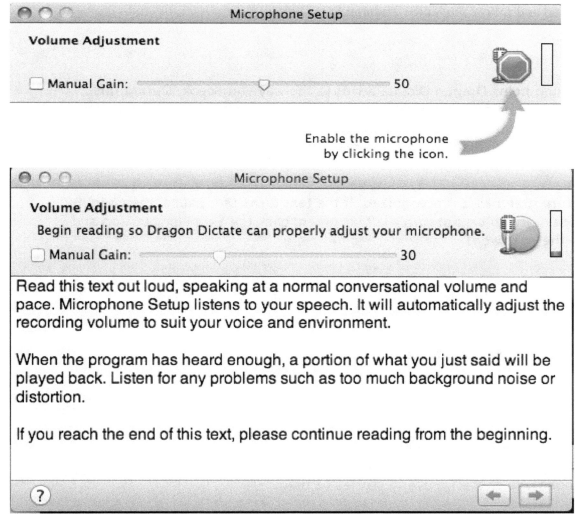

YOU MAY NEED TO READ THESE PARGRAPHS SEVERAL TIMES before the following message appears. On this screen, you may automatically hear your voice being played back or you can click play. (See steps for Voice Training on the next page).

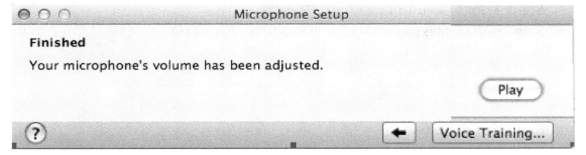

1.3 Voice Training

When you are creating a profile for the first time, you will be required to do voice training. This is where Dragon Dictate listens to your speech to determine how *your* voice sounds and how *you* pronounce your words. It is important to read in your normal speaking voice with the volume you will usually use. Read and follow the Voice Training Steps below.

○ ○ ○   Voice Training

Voice Training helps Dragon Dictate adapt to the way you speak. During this process, you will be asked to read a story, including punctuation. This should take you five minutes or less. The training process will stop when enough speech has been collected, usually before you reach the end of the story.

Text will turn green as it is recognized. If the text turns red, pause, then begin reading again. If you cannot turn the text green, click the Skip Word button and start with the next word.

The progress bar on the panel will show how far along you are in the story.

Click the right arrow to continue.

○ ○ ○   Voice Training

The program needs to hear your voice to give you the best recognition results. Please choose one of the following stories to read.

Welcome (Easier Reading: Instructional)
Children's Stories (Reading for Children)
Stage Fright (Medium Reading: Humor)
Sales E-mail Messages (Medium Reading: Business)

Click the right arrow to continue.

Enable the microphone by clicking the icon and start reading the story.

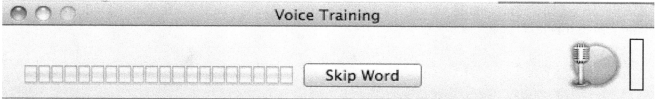

Notice the text should turn green as you progress…if it turns red and goes back to black you need to repeat the text. After you read a few screens, you will get the following message. This may take several seconds to process.

Performing Initial Calibration...

Voice Training

Dragon Dictate has collected enough speech to perform training. You do not have to read the entire story.

After processing is complete, you will be ready to dictate into all your favorite Macintosh applications.

You may return to Voice Training and read more stories to improve Dragon Dictate's ability to recognize your voice by selecting "Voice Training..." from the "Tools" menu.

Processing Training...

Voice Training

Voice Training is complete.

You may return to Voice Training and read more stories to improve Dragon Dictate's ability to recognize your voice. To read more stories, select "Voice Training..." from the "Tools" menu.

Click Done

The following welcome screen and interactive tutorial will appear. Click on Tutorial and complete the interactive exercises. These are introductory lessons. You will learn more features and become more comfortable with using speech recognition as you work though the additional chapters in this text.

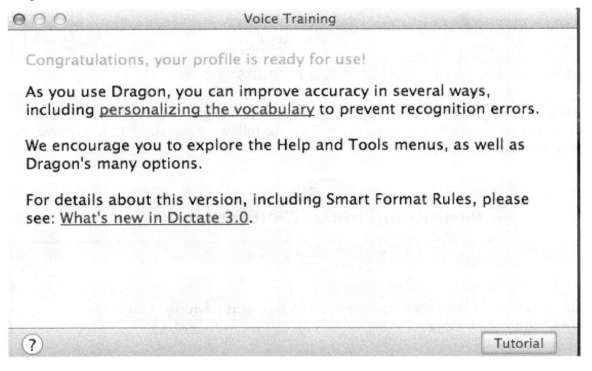

What's next?

You have now completed the Interactive Tutorial. Of course, there is much more to Dragon than what you saw in these lessons.

As you start using Dragon, focus on practicing good dictation habits and getting used to composing out loud. Be sure to take advantage of the items under the Tools menu to personalize and enhance your profile.

Over time, you can learn to do more and more by voice.

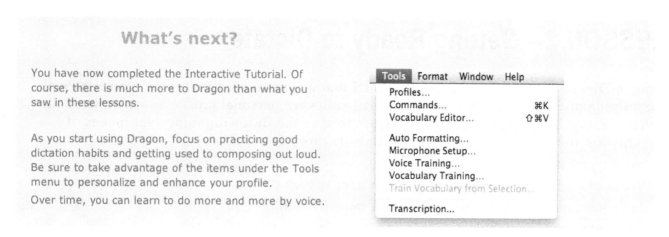

1.4 Quitting Dragon Dictate and Saving Your Profile

Dragon Dictate actually learns how you speak and compensates for misrecognitions and your regional accent as you use the software. Your profile accuracy will continue to improve each time you use it and Dragon Dictate will automatically update and save your voice profile when you choose **Quit Dictate**. (There is a separate **Save Profile** command under the **File** menu for those who may want a "safety valve" to make certain that changes in the profile are not lost in case of a power failure or similar unforeseen event). However, most users just use the automatic saving.

Go to the **Dictate** menu and Choose **Quit Dictate** to close your newly created profile. You will practice reopening your profile in the next Chapter.

LESSON 2—Getting Ready to Dictate

Dragon Dictate has an internal speech model that adapts to each individual voice through the training process. In Lesson 1, you created your own personal profile and completed the voice training. This allows Dragon Dictate™ to save the following important pieces of information for you every time you use the software:

- Audio settings
- Acoustic information gathered to learn user speech patterns
- Information about any words that have been trained
- User-generated vocabulary words or phrases
- Word usage information
- Settings changed in the Options dialog box
- Custom voice commands

In this chapter, you will become familiar with many of the Dragon Dictate components that will help you customize your profile further to increase your overall dictation recognition and accuracy.

2.1 Opening Dragon Dictate

Follow these steps to Open your User Profile, Setup Microphone and view Status Window.

- Start Dragon Dictate by clicking on the Dragon icon or choose Go, Applications, Dragon Dictate.

- Select your profile and click Continue

Dragon Dictate

When you first open your profile, you may be prompted to set up your microphone automatically or you may see **one** or **more** of the following windows: **Microphone Setup, Status Window** or **Notepad.** (Don't be concerned if all of these do not open automatically. You will learn more about each of these windows throughout this chapter).

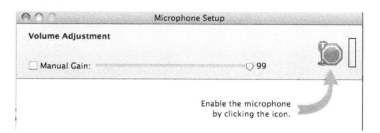

Microphone Setup

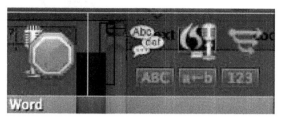

Dragon Status Window

Dragon Notepad

2.2 Microphone Tips

The Microphone Setup is very important. Start by checking the position of your headset. Make sure you place your headset in a comfortable position with the tip of the microphone being about 3/4 of an inch away from your lower lip, and, if possible, move it slightly to the side so it is not directly in front of your mouth. This helps avoid breathing errors. Keeping the microphone in the same position helps your speech recognition performance. (**Tools, Microphone Setup** allows you to test your headset by adjusting your volume. This is also known as tuning your microphone.)

1) Test your headset on a daily basis. Retest your microphone any time you feel you are getting less accuracy than you should. Testing your Microphone can compensate for many things that can affect the way Dragon Dictate hears.

2) Avoid touching or holding the microphone tip—the part of the microphone you speak into.

3) Move the microphone tip slightly further away from your mouth if extra words appear on the screen caused by your breathing.

4) Keep your chin slightly elevated when you speak, as if you are talking to a person. Don't talk down into your chest or mumble.

5) If audio problems persist, try plugging the headset into a different port or test it on a different computer. Audio problems may be the result of a defective headset.

6) Keep your microphone OFF when you are not talking to the computer.

2.3 Microphone Setup

If your Microphone Setup window did not open automatically when you opened your profile, Go to **Tools** on the Dragon Dictate Menu Bar and choose > **Microphone Setup** OR turn on your microphone and say **"Show Microphone Setup"** to adjust your volume. Click done when you volume has been adjusted.

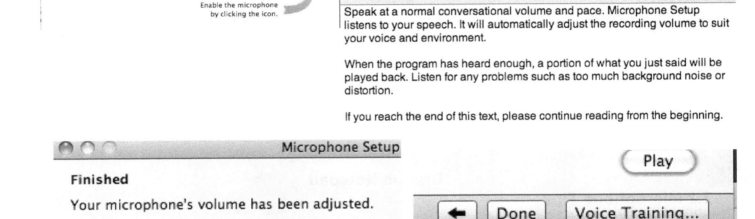

2.4 Microphone Commands

Beginners with speech recognition stumble because they simply do not control the microphone. Turning the microphone on and off is as simple as:

- Click the microphone icon on the status window
- On Dragon Dictate Bar, choose **Speech**, **Microphone On**
- Click Microphone on or off from the Dock
- Saying MICROPHONE OFF
- Pressing the keyboard shortcut—"hot key"

The microphone needs to be turned off/or hibernated when NOT dictating. Unlike a passive keyboard, which is waiting to be pressed into action, the microphone is an active device. It is best to turn the **microphone off** when not speaking to your computer. However, you may also put the microphone in **hibernation** mode by saying **SLEEP MODE** or **GO TO SLEEP.** When the microphone is in hibernation mode, it is actually still ON and is waiting for a voice command. Some people have problems with the microphone turning itself back on before they are ready. Therefore, it is recommended the microphone be turned off verses hibernating.

The following exercises gives you practice with using Microphone Commands.

2.5 Microphone Activation Commands

1. The Status Window indicates if the microphone is ON, OFF or in SLEEP MODE. One way to turn the microphone ON or OFF is to click or tap on the Microphone icon on the Status Window. The icon will be red when the microphone is OFF and green when the microphone is ON.

2. Other ways to turn your microphone ON or OFF include:

Using Dragon Dictate Speech Menu   or   Dictate Dock options

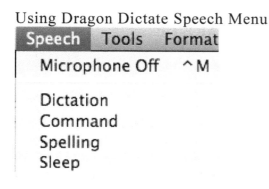 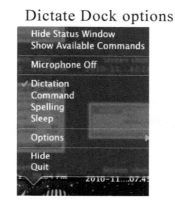

3. You can also turn the microphone OFF by voice: Say • MICROPHONE OFF. This command turns your microphone completely off. (NOTE: The microphone CANNOT be turned on with a voice command when the microphone is completely off.)

4. Set a keyboard shortcut "hot key". Go to Dictate, Preferences and click on Shortcuts. Next to Toggle Microphone, press your shortcut keys. In this example, Control M is set as the shortcut.

5. Try each of these Microphone Activation Options to determine how you would like to control your microphone.

2.6 Microphone Hibernation Commands

The dot (•) reminds you to be silent for 1/2 second before saying a command. **Hibernating your microphone puts the microphone in a pause mode so you can talk to others and then reactivate the microphone by voice. (Try the following)**

1. Turn on the microphone by clicking the icon. Say **•SLEEP MODE. (Notice microphone icon on Status Window changes to a blue moon)**

2. To wake your microphone from hibernation, say **• WAKE UP.**

3. Practice hibernating the microphone and pay attention to the icon in the **Status Window**.

2.7 Commands vs. Dictation

Talking to your computer may seem awkward at first. Remember, you are learning a new skill. Be patient and take the time to work through the step-by-step activities throughout this book. This will help you become more comfortable using speech recognition software and will help Dragon Dictate get to know your unique voice.

The first thing you need to understand is the difference between <u>dictating</u> and giving a <u>command</u>. **Dictating** is when you want the computer to type what you say. A **command** is when you are telling the computer to perform a task. It is not necessary to learn a lot of commands to begin with. The activities throughout this book will help you become more familiar with dictating and using voice commands. **Don't try to do everything with your voice.**

It is OK to use your voice, keyboard or mouse. However, you will find that voice input should be much faster in many instances. If it is easier for you to use your keyboard or mouse to open/close programs, navigate or format documents then use these devices. Again, be patient and give yourself and the computer time to become more precise.

LESSON 3—Dragon Dictate Modes and Commands

3.1 Dragon Status Window

The **status window** is your control center for Dragon Dictate. It floats over the windows of all other applications. Here you can turn the microphone on and off, change modes, and get a better idea of how Dragon Dictate is responding to your voice.

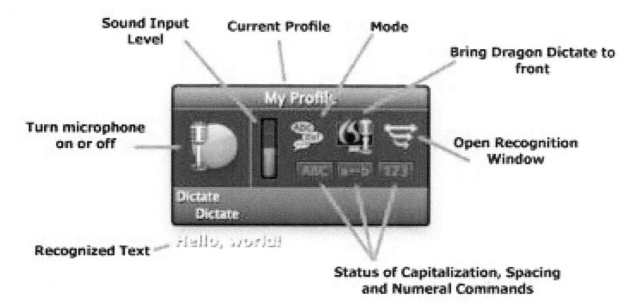

TIPS

- Be sure the name of your profile shows where this says "My Profile" especially if you share your computer with other users. (Each person needs to set up their own unique profile).

- Keep your microphone off when you are not speaking to the computer.

- If sound input level is in the red. Go to Tools, Microphone Setup and test your microphone.

- The **Dictate Mode** is the most flexible mode and easiest to use.

- **Bring Dragon Dictate to Front** activates the Dragon Dictate menu. This menu needs to be active in order for the computer to process any of your voice commands.

- **Recognized Text** displays how Dragon recognizes your command or dictation. It is especially helpful when giving a command. If Dragon misinterprets the command, it will not be able to perform the action. If you noticed Dragon misinterpreted your command, just repeat the command again and you will often notice it will appear correctly.

You will learn more about each of the Status Window features as you continue working through additional lessons.

3.2 Dragon Dictate Modes and Menu Bar

Dragon Dictate has four modes. Each mode has different settings that determine how Dragon Dictate will respond to your speech. The indicator on the Status Window changes according to what Mode is activated. **(You will stay in the DICTATION MODE for most of your activities).**

 DICTATION MODE—Dragon Dictate can interpret both commands and dictation. If your words are interpreted as a command, it obeys the command. Otherwise, Dragon Dictate will type your words at the insertion point in the front-most application. This is the most common mode.

 COMMAND MODE—Dragon Dictate interprets your words only as commands. This mode is useful when you want to issue a series of commands and want to make sure that nothing you say is accidentally typed into your document.

 SPELLING MODE--Dragon Dictate tries to interpret your words as a limited set of letters and punctuation, and types those letters and punctuation at the insertion point in the foremost document. inThis mode is useful for Web addresses or whenever you want to spell out words.

 SLEEP MODE—Hibernates your microphone. You used the **SLEEP MODE** in the previous exercise by saying "Go to Sleep" or "Sleep Mode".

Turn on your Microphone and practice switching between modes. Watch the Status Window Indicator change.

- Say •**SLEEP MODE,** •**WAKE UP**

- Say •**COMMAND MODE,** •**DICTATION MODE**

- SAY •**SPELLING MODE,** •**DICTATION MODE**

Dictate Menu Bar

The **Dragon Dictate Menu Bar** contains menus that are specific to the Dragon program when it is active.

Since Dragon Dictate is designed to operate in the background while you dictate into your favorite applications, it is sometimes easy for it to seem hidden in the background. You can tell if Dragon Dictate is running if you see its **Status window** on your screen. The **Dictate menu bar** must be showing in order to use the Dragon menus. The quickest way to activate this menu bar is to click on the "Bring Dragon Dictate to front" icon shown on the Status Window or say "**Show dictate**" or "**Bring dictate to the front**". (*Remember to be able to use any Dragon Dictate Commands the Dictate menu must be showing*).

3.3 Command Basics

There are many specific commands built into Dragon Dictate. However, there are only a few commands that most people use on a daily basis. As a beginner, it is important to learn the basics before trying to memorize a lot of commands.

BASIC COMMAND TIPS

- There are six categories of commands.

- Commands become more natural and easier to use the more you use speech recognition software and become comfortable talking to your computer.

- Commands can be edited, modified, created, activated and deactivated once you become more advanced with speech recognition software.

- Commands should only be used when they are faster than using the keyboard or mouse.

- Commands are often use to open or close menus and applications, navigate, and format documents.

- Dragon Dictate understands multiple-word commands better than just one word.

- Pause slightly before and after giving a command.

BEGINNING COMMANDS TO LEARN

Go To Sleep	Hibernates Microphone
Microphone Off	Turns off Microphone
Bring Dictate to Front or Show Dictate	Activates Dictate Menu Bar (Must be showing in order to use the Dragon menus)
Show or Access <menu item>	Displays menu choice
Open or Quit <application>	Opens or quits whatever application you name
New or Next Line	Presses enter key once
New or Next Paragraph	Presses enter key twice
Tab Key	Indents Paragraph
Go to Beginning or End	Moves cursor to beginning or end of document
Insert before or after <word or phrase>	Moves cursor to specific location
Select <word or phrase>	Used to identify text that a command is going to be applied to.

Lessons 3.4 and 3.5 give you some practice using some of these basic commands. You will learn more about commands and the command features in Lessons 8 and 9.

3.4 Window and Menu Activation Commands

You already practiced saying the microphone and mode commands: " Microphone Off", "Go To Sleep", "Wake Up", "Sleep Mode", "Normal Mode", "Dictation Mode" and "Command Mode". Now you will practice using other Window and Program activation commands.

- Say •**BRNG DICTATE TO FRONT** to show Dictate menu bar

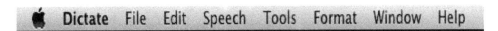

You can choose **any** of your available Dictate menus by voice by using the " SHOW" or " ACCESS" command before the name of the menu item.

- Say •**HIDE STATUS WINDOW** this removes the Status Window icon from the desktop.

- Say •**SHOW STATUS WINDOW** to have it reappear.

- Repeat the Hide and Show Status Window commands to Hide then Show the Status Window. Notice when the Status window is hidden, you would need to look for the microphone icons on the Tool bars to see if the microphone is on or off.

(If you have trouble voicing any of these commands, remember you can also choose the item from the Dictate Bar, Window)

- Say •**SHOW AVAILABLE COMMANDS** or choose from Dictate Bar, Window.

- Say •**HIDE AVAILABLE COMMANDS** or click the close box to close this window.

> You will learn more about the commands features in Lesson 8 and 9.

3.5 Program Activation Commands

- To open programs by voice say "**OPEN** and the name of the program". To close a program, say "**QUIT** and the name of the program.

- Don't hesitate between saying the word OPEN or QUIT and the name of the program.

- If a program doesn't open or quit when giving the voice command, look at the Recognition Text on the Status Bar. Dragon may not have recognized the command. You may have to repeat the command or just open or quit the program with your keyboard or mouse.

▪ Say • **OPEN TEXT EDIT**

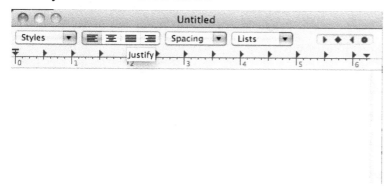

▪ Say •**QUIT TEXT EDIT**

▪ Say •OPEN **MICROSOFT WORD**. (If Microsoft Word is on your computer, it will open.)

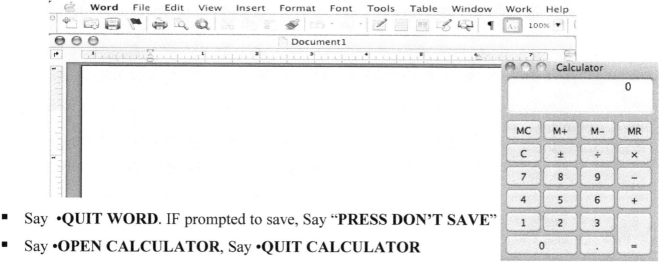

▪ Say •**QUIT WORD**. IF prompted to save, Say "**PRESS DON'T SAVE**"

▪ Say •**OPEN CALCULATOR**, Say •**QUIT CALCULATOR**

▪ Say •**OPEN SAFARI**, Say •**QUIT SAFARI** (or browser of your choice…Firefox, Internet Explorer)

Practice voicing the **OPEN** and **QUIT** commands to open and quit other programs that you may use on a regular basis.

LESSON 4—Dictation Basics

When first starting to use speech recognition software, many people find it easier to read something to the computer instead of composing or dictating from scratch. The more you talk to the computer in your natural speaking voice the better the software will recognize your unique speech patterns and dialect.

4.1 Dictating Tips

- Do NOT watch your screen as you dictate and do NOT try to correct your errors as you speak. Say what you're going to say, and don't worry about misrecognized words or mistakes. (You'll learn how to correct these later.)

- Speak naturally at your normal speed. Pronounce each word clearly, not loudly, and in a way that is comfortable for you.

- Say each word ending clearly. For example, and say something not ansay somethin'.

- Do not speak too deliberately! Keep words together. Do not speak in syllables. For example, say conversations. Do not say, con verse say shuns. If you find yourself breaking words into syllables, slightly pick up the pace of your speaking.

- For best recognition, speak in longer phrases rather than short phrases or individual words. This helps with fluency and allows Dragon to run a grammar/statistical check of your sentences, thereby improving accuracy.

- Dictate all punctuation marks.

Have patience and think of ways that you can practice talking to your computer:

The more you practice talking to your computer, the more comfortable you will become and the more naturally you will speak. You can practice a little each day by reading something out loud to the computer.

Think about some things you may be planning to read over the next few days. For example, if you are going to read a newspaper article, instead of reading it silently to yourself, activate your speech recognition software and read the article out loud into Dragon Notepad or another text application.

Practicing tips: Don't think about reading to your computer. Just read the article without looking at your screen. Don't worry about mistakes. It is okay if you stumble over words or the computer doesn't understand everything you say. You are practicing talking out loud to your computer and the speech recognition software is recording how you speak to improve your overall recognition and accuracy.

4.2 Dragon Notepad

You can dictate into virtually any Macintosh application. If a program has an area into which you would normally type, you will probably be able to speak and Dragon Dictate will type for you. Please understand that some applications accept dictation more readily than others.

Dragon Dictate also comes with its own **built-in word processor** — Note Pad. The Note Pad window is a word processing window that is specifically aimed at dictation through Dragon Dictate. It is recommended to use the Note Pad window when first dictating information. Once your dictation is complete, the text can be easily be copied and pasted into your working document. Note Pad window contents are also saved as .rtf files which can be opened for editing later with another word processor (TextEdit, Microsoft Word, etc.) in addition to Notepad.

The Notepad Window may open automatically when you choose your profile. However, you should follow these steps when you want to open a New Notepad window.

- Say •**BRING DICTATE TO FRONT** to show Dictate menu bar
  (you can also click on the dictate icon on the Status Window).

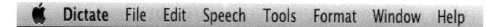

- Say •**CREATE NEW NOTEPAD** to open a new Notepad with your *voice (you can also choose New Notepad under the File menu with your mouse.)*

The text in the Notepad window may be hard to see. To set the default font and size for a brand-new Notepad window, choose format > font> show font, specify the desired font and size OR use Bigger and Smaller to adjust size.

- Say **Welcome to speech recognition PERIOD** *(Don't worry if Dragon makes mistakes. You will learn to correct errors later.)*

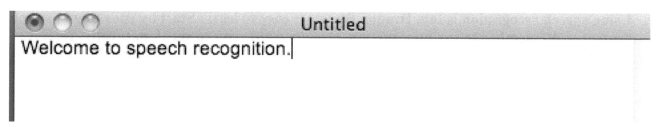

- Say •**FILE CLOSE** (or use mouse)

- Say •**PRESS DON'T SAVE (**or click don't save)

4.3 Practice Dictating, Selecting and Deleting Text

*Say punctuation marks like • **PERIOD.***

1. Turn on your Microphone. Make sure the Dictate Bar is active by saying •SHOW DICTATE

2. Say •**CREATE NEW NOTE PAD** to open a new notepad

3. After your program opens, dictate the following (do not pay attention to errors or try to make corrections):

    Using speech recognition is fun PERIOD Dragon Dictate is easy to learn PERIOD Start by speaking in simple sentences PERIOD Remember to say punctuation PERIOD Dragon wants you to speak naturally PERIOD Do not stop between words or break words into syllables PERIOD Speak to your computer the way television news personalities read the news PERIOD

4. Hibernate your microphone by saying **SLEEP MODE or GO TO SLEEP**

5. Count your mistakes. If you made five or less errors, you have achieved 90 percent accuracy or better.

6. Turn your microphone **ON** by saying **WAKE UP or TURN MICROPHONE ON**

7. Say • **SELECT ALL** to select all of the text.

8. Say • **DELETE SELECTION** to erase screen.

9. For practice, repeat the dialogue again. Say • **PERIOD** as needed.

    Using speech recognition is fun. Dragon Dictate is easy to learn. Start by speaking in simple sentences. Remember to say punctuation. Dragon wants you to speak naturally. Do not stop between words or break words into syllables. Speak to your computer the way television news personalities read the news.

10. Hibernate your microphone by saying **SLEEP MODE or GO TO SLEEP**

11. Count your mistakes. If you made five or less errors, you have achieved 90 percent accuracy or better.

12. Turn your microphone **ON** by saying **WAKE UP or TURN MICROPHONE ON**

13. Exit Notepad by saying • **CLOSE WINDOW**

---

14. Say •**PRESS DON'T SAVE** to exit without saving.

Use the • **NEW LINE** command when you need to make a line break. This is the same as pressing the Enter Key once. Use the • **NEW PARAGRAPH** command to create a double space, this is like pressing the Enter Key twice.

Tip: When dictating, say these commands sharply after a • 1/2 second of complete silence.

- **NEW LINE**   not   • **NEW LiiyNE**
- **NEW PARAGRAPH**   not   • **NEW PARAGRaa**

  If you have trouble with these commands, you can say PRESS ENTER or press your Enter key on the keyboard.

Speech recognition software also allows you to say your punctuation marks and place them exactly where you want them to go. Look at the following examples:

- Say • **COMMA for** ,
- Say • **EXCLAMATION MARK** or • **EXCLAMATION POINT for** !
- Say • **COLON for** :
- Say • **SEMICOLON for** ;

4.4   Practice New Paragraph & New Line

While practicing the • NEW LINE and • NEW PARAGRAPH commands, do not be too bring dictation to front bring dictation to front concerned about correcting your dictation errors. You'll learn to make corrections later!

1.   Turn on your microphone if it is off. If you have closed Notepad, open the program once again.

2.   Speak the following dialogue. Remember to say punctuation marks and pause a second or two (•) before saying commands. *If you make a few mistakes, ignore them for this exercise:* *

Wow! I get to go on a trip to Australia. • NEW PARAGRAPH
The Australian outback is full of animals. • NEW PARAGRAPH
The animals include: (NEW LINE)
kangaroos (NEW LINE)
crocodiles (NEW LINE)
snakes (NEW PARAGRAPH)

Kangaroos live in the Australian outback. (NEW LINE)
Crocodiles live in the swamp. (NEW LINE)
Snakes live in the trees. (NEW LINE)

*Notice if you say a punctuation mark at the end of the sentence or say NEW PARAGRAPH, the next word is automatically capitalized. If you say NEW LINE, without a punctuation mark at the end of the line, the next word will not be capitalized – the software considers the new line to be a continuation of the same sentence. Look at animal list above.

3.   Say • **FILE CLOSE**
4.   Say • **PRESS DON'T SAVE**

4.5   Practice Dictating—Speak Clearly & Delete All

1. Turn on your Microphone. Say •**SHOW DICTATE** (pause) Say •**CREATE NEW NOTE PAD.**

2. After your program opens, dictate the following two paragraphs saying all punctuation marks and New Paragraph command. (Do not pay attention to errors or try to make corrections):

   We are learning how to dictate using speech recognition software. This software allows us to use our voice in addition to the keyboard or mouse to create documents. The computer will type what we dictate or do what we command as we dictate words, numbers, symbols and a variety of formatting commands. (NEW PARAGRAPH)
   We will learn what commands to use and how to train the computer to recognize our unique voices by completing exercises in this training manual. Once we have learned some basics, we will use the speech recognition software to create many different documents including emails, letters, reports, and spreadsheets.

3. Say •**MICROPHONE OFF** to turn off your microphone

4. Count your mistakes. Since there are 100 words in these two paragraphs each mistake is subtracted from 100 to determine your accuracy rate. Example: If you had five errors, your accuracy is 95%. Remember, your accuracy levels will improve the more you use the software.

5. Click close with your mouse to close this Note Pad file and don't SAVE.

4.6   Voice Training to Improve Accuracy

You most likely speak between 110 and 180 words per minute. Everyone has their own natural speaking speed. Remember, **accuracy** is more important than speed. If you try to talk much faster or much slower than you normally speak your accuracy will be lower.

As mentioned at the beginning of this chapter, one of the best ways to improve your speech recognition accuracy is to practice reading out loud to the computer. Dragon Dictate has additional built-in stories that you can read to help improve your overall accuracy. If your accuracy is not continuously improving over time, you may want to read additional text passages by following the steps below:

Go to the **Tools menu** on the **Dictate Bar** and **choose Voice Training** (You can also do this by voice by turning on your microphone and saying **SHOW VOICE TRAINING WINDOW.**

Voice Training helps Dragon Dictate adapt to the way you speak. During this process, you will be asked to read a story, including punctuation. This should take you five minutes or less. The training process will stop when enough speech has been collected, usually before you reach the end of the story.

Text will turn green as it is recognized. If the text turns red, pause, then begin reading again. If you cannot turn the text green, click the Skip Word button and start with the next word.

Select one of the three stories and read the paragraphs in your normal speaking voice.

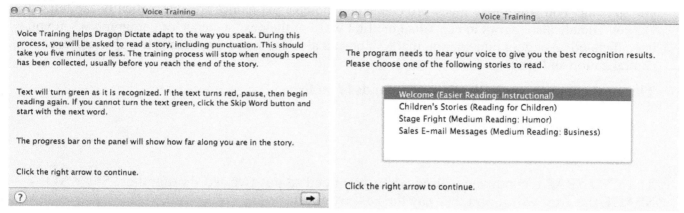

Remember, the text will go from black to green if it recognizes your voice. Otherwise, the text will turn to red and you will need to repeat.

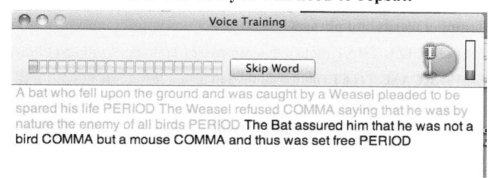

When enough information has been collected, you will receive the following message.

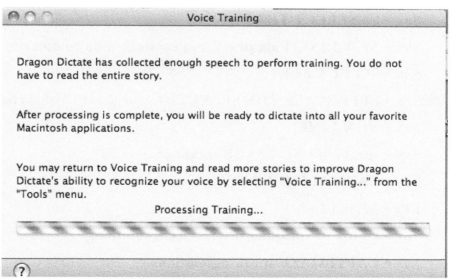

4.7 Capitalization & Compounding Words

Dragon Dictate comes with a large vocabulary of built-in words that includes correct capitalization and spacing. You will notice many pro create new notepadper names are automatically capitalized. Dragon Dictate also knows to capitalize the first word of the next sentence or paragraph when you have dictated an ending punctuation mark. You can also use voice commands to apply correct capitalization and spacing.

The most common capitalization commands include:
- **CAPITALIZE**
- **LOWERCASE**
- **UPPERCASE**

The • **NO SPACE** command is used when you need to put two words together. Say • **NO SPACE** the first word, and then say the next word.

- **Open a New Notepad and complete the following exercise to practice capitalization and spacing commands.** (Don't worry if Dragon makes mistakes, you are just practicing the capitalization and spacing feature for this exercise)

  Say • **Training words and phrases**

  Say • **CAPITALIZE THAT** (notice this capitalizes Training Word and Phrases)

  Say • **LOWERCASE THAT** (notice all the letters are lowercase now)

  Say • **UPPERCASE THAT**

  Say • **NEW LINE Using natural capitalization**

  Say • **CAPITALIZE Natural**

  Say • **UPPERCASE Capitalization**

  Say • **SELECT using natural capitalization**

  Say • **UNSELECT THAT**

  Say • **NEW LINE I am practicing capitalization commands**

  Say • **SELECT ALL**

  Say • **UPPERCASE THE SELECTION** (be sure to include the word the)

  Say • NEW LINE

  Say • **speaking** • **NO SPACE solutions**

  Say • **CAPITALIZE THAT**

  Say • **NEW LINE**

  Say • I work at **speaking** • **NO SPACE solutions**

  Say • **CAPTIALIZE speakingsolutions**

Repeat this exercise to get additional practice with these commands. Quit Notepad and don't save.

LESSON 5—Selecting and Dictating

Remember, when you are first learning to use speech recognition software, it is important to follow the proper dictating tips and practice dictating without worrying about any mistakes. Not only will you become more comfortable in talking to the computer, the software will actually learn how you speak and compensate for mispronunciations and your regional accent.

5.1 Selecting Words by Voice

To make corrections, you will often need to select the text first. You could select the text with your mouse or keyboard. However, it is more efficient to use the **SELECT** command.

The voice command to select a word or phrase is **SELECT <text>** (<text> is the word or phrase you want to select) or you can say **SELECT <text> THROUGH <text>** to select a word or phrase at the beginning and at the end of the range you want to select.

Remember the moment of silence (•) before you say the • **SELECT** command. However, DO NOT hesitate after you say the • **SELECT** command.

Practice using the SELECT and UNSELECT command by completing the following steps:

1) Open a new window by saying: **CREATE NEW NOTEPAD**

2) Dictate sentence: **George Washington was the first president of the United States.**

3) Say • **SELECT George Washington** (Notice George Washington is selected)

George Washington was the first president of the United States.

4) Say • **UNSELECT THAT**

5) Say • **SELECT first through States**

George Washington was the first president of the United States.

6) Say • **UNSELECT THAT**

7) **Say** •**SELECT ALL**

8) **Say** • **DELETE SELECTION** to clear document

Continue to practice the **SELECT command by** dictating the following paragraphs. (Again, don't worry about any mistakes. You are just practicing the **SELECT command** for now.)

Dictate:

James went to the university to get an education. He went to class almost every day. After school he went to work. There was very little time to play.

1) Say • **SELECT time to play.**

2) Say • **SELECT After school.**

3) Say • **SELECT went to class.**

4) Say •**SELECT ALL**

5) Say • **DELETE SELECTION** to clear document

Dictate the following paragraph:

Using speech recognition is fun. Dragon Dictate is easy to learn. Start by speaking in simple sentences. Remember to say punctuation. Dragon wants you to speak naturally. Do not stop between words or break words into syllables. Speak to your computer the way television news personalities read the news.

1) SELECT "fun"

   Using·speech·recognition·is·fun.·Dragon·NaturallySpeaking·is·easy·to·learn.·Start·by·speaking·in·simple·

2) SELECT "Using speech recognition is fun"

   ¶
   Using·speech·recognition·is·fun.·Dragon·NaturallySpeaking·is·easy·to·learn.·Start·by·speaking·in·simple·

3) SELECT "Using speech THROUGH simple" (This allows you to select a block of text).

   ¶
   Using·speech·recognition·is·fun.·Dragon·NaturallySpeaking·is·easy·to·learn.·Start·by·speaking·in·simple·
   sentences.·Remember·to·say·punctuation.· select line n·wants·you·to·speak·naturally.·Do·not·stop·between·

4) SELECT ALL

   ¶
   Using·speech·recognition·is·fun.·Dragon·NaturallySpeaking·is·easy·to·learn.·Start·by·speaking·in·simple·
   sentences.·Remember·to·say·punctuation.·Dragon·wants·you·to·speak·naturally.·Do·not·stop·between·
   words·or·break·words·into·s select paragraph peak·to·your·computer·the·way·television·news·personalities·
   read·the·news.¶

5) UNSELECT THAT

Words and phrases need to be **SELECTED** before they can be edited or formatted. It is important to become comfortable with using the **SELECT COMMAND** because it is one of the most useful commands when using Dragon Dictate.

5.2 Select Again, Select Next and Select Previous

Speech recognition is a phrase technology. If you speak in phrases your software can run grammar and word frequency statistics to improve accuracy. It is the same with selecting. It is easier to select a phrase than it is to select individual words. It is often better to **SELECT** the word you want including the word before or after it especially if there are multiple occurrences of the word.

Dragon Dictate selects the closest instance of a word then selects the next words moving forward through your document until it reaches the end. You can move to another instance of the same word by saying • **SELECT AGAIN, SELECT PREVIOUS,** or **SELECT NEXT.**

1) Be sure your cursor is at the beginning of a New NotePad document and the Dictate Menu is showing. (If not, remember to Say •**SHOW DICTATE** and •**FILE NEW NOTE PAD**)

2) Now dictate the following paragraph:

   James went to the University to get an education. He went to class almost every day. After school he went to work. There was very little time to play.

3) Use your mouse to move your cursor to the beginning of the document. (Later you will learn voice commands to move cursor).

4) Say • **SELECT TO** to choose the last instance of the word "**to.**"

James went to the University to get an education. He went to class I missed every day. After school he went to work. There was very little

5) Say • **SELECT AGAIN** to choose the very next instance of the word "**to.**"

James went to the University to get an education. He went to class I missed every day. After school he went to work. There was very little

6) Say • **SELECT NEXT** to choose the next instance of the word "**to.**"

James went to the University to get an education. He went to class I missed every day. After school he went to work. There was very little

7) Say • **SELECT PREVIOUS** to go back to the previous instance of the word "**to.**"

James went to the University to get an education. He went to class I missed everv dav. After school he went to work. There was verv little

8) Say • **SELECT** "to play" notice this jumped to the last instance of **to** because both of the words "to play" were selected.

> James went to the University to get an education. He went to class I missed every day. After school he went to work. There was very little time to play.

9) Practice using **SELECT**, **SELECT AGAIN**, **SELECT PREVIOUS** and **SELECT NEXT** to become more comfortable with these commands.

5.3 Selecting and Replacing Words by Voice

One way to make corrections by voice is to use the **SELECT and SAY** method. This is where you select the misrecognized word or phrase and then say the correct word or phrase to be replaced.

1) Dictate the sentence: George Washington was the first president of the United States.

2) Say • **SELECT George Washington**

3) Say • **Thomas Jefferson**. (Thomas Jefferson will replace George Washington in the sentence.)

4) Say • **SELECT first president.**

> ◉ ○ ○   Untitled
> Thomas Jefferson was the first president of the United States.

5) Say • **third president.**

6) Say • **SELECT Thomas Jefferson.**

> ◉ ○ ○   Untitled
> Thomas Jefferson was the third president of the United States.

7) Say • **John Adams.**

8) **SELECT** • **third president.**

9) Say • **second president.**

> ◉ ○ ○   Untitled
> John Adams was the second| president of the United States.

10) Say • **SELECT ALL** (*pause*) **DELETE SELECTION** to clear screen.

If you have trouble selecting words with your voice or Dragon is still misrecognizing what you are saying, just use the keyboard and mouse to correct any errors for now.

5.4 Practice Dictating and Using Select and Say

Dictate the following paragraphs and practice using the "Select and Say" to make corrections. Remember to dictate the entire paragraph before selecting and correcting any of the mistakes. DO NOT try to correct as you dictate.

1. Turn on your microphone. Say • **SHOW DICTATE,** • **FILE NEW NOTEPAD** to open a blank Notepad.

2. Dictate the following paragraph:

   People have the ability to carry on conversations and tell stories. Almost everyone can relate to a story and say something meaningful. Today they have the software to convert their speech into typed text.

3. Correct any mistakes using the **SELECT and SAY.** (Review the steps in the previous exercise if necessary).

4. Say• **GO TO END to move cursor to end of paragraph**

5. Say "**NEW PARAGRAPH**"

6. Now try this more complex paragraph. Be sure to say the hyphen between the words *voice* and *writing* in the following way: *voice hyphen writing. (Pre-reading the paragraph in your mind before speaking will help you smooth out the rough spots in your mind before you start to speak.)*

   Voice-writing requires practice and lots of it. People adjust the pace of their writing to the efficiency of their input tools. In centuries past, writers would saddle their thoughts and slowed them down to a walk when crafting paragraphs with paper and pencil.

7. Again, select and correct any mistakes in this paragraph using the **SELECT and SAY.**

8. Say • **GO TO END** if your cursor is not at the end of the paragraph. Say • **NEW PARAGRAPH**

9. Dictate the final paragraph:

   Eventually, writers learned to type and entered their thoughts into typing machines at a trot, or even a gallop, to the rhythmic tapping of their fingers across the keyboard. By comparison, voice-writers produce copy at a run. Learning to think, compose, speak clearly, and edit at the speed of speech takes effort and rehearsal.

10. Again, select and correct any mistakes in this final paragraph using the **SELECT** and **SAY.**

11. Keep this document open and follow the steps for **Saving Documents with Your Voice** on the next page.

5.5 Saving Documents with Your Voice

- To **Save** a Dragon Notepad document, Say **SAVE DOCUMENT** or use your mouse to click file, save.

- Use your mouse to navigate to the location where you would like to save your file. In this example, a folder named My Exercises was created in Documents.

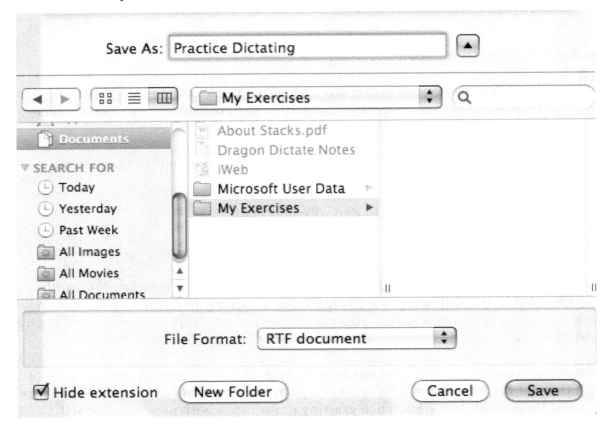

- With the cursor in the **Save As** box, you can use your voice (or keyboard) to name your document. Notice Notepad saves the file as a RTF document.

- Say • **Practice Dictating** (*don't worry if it is not capitalized*)

- Say • **PRESS SAVE** or click the save button to save the file.

- To Print Say •**SHOW PRINT** and Say •**PRESS PRINT** (*or you can choose and click print by hand*)

LESSON 6—Correcting

Most of the time it is best to dictate then go back and use the **Select and Say** to make corrections. However, there are some quick correction commands that you can use if you know that you have misspoken or wish to erase the last phrase or phrases you have spoken.

6.1 Quick Correction Commands

• **DELETE SELECTION**– erases "selected" text

• **SCRATCH THAT** or **SCRATCH WORD**– erases the last spoken group of words or word.

• **UNDO LAST ACTION** or **REDO LAST ACTION**– erases or restores last dictation or removes or restores last command. (Can also replace **LAST ACTION** with **DICTATION**)

• **INSERT BEFORE** or **INSERT AFTER**– quickly moves cursor to specific location .

Open a **New Notepad** and dictate the following paragraph and practice the • **DELETE,** • **SCRATCH,** • **UNDO, INSERT BEFORE** and **INSERT AFTER** commands.

Speech recognition is better than I imagined. I can now type as fast as I can talk. I know I must create a profile, adjust my microphone and perform an audio check before I can begin using speech recognition.

1. Say • **SCRATCH THAT** to erase the words you said after your last pause.

2. Say • **UNDO THAT** to cancel the **SCRATCH THAT** command and bring the erased words back.

3. Say • **SCRATCH WORD** to erase just one word to the left of the cursor.

4. Dictate the last sentence again without stopping between any words. (Notice when you say •**SCRATCH THAT**, the entire line is erased).

5. Dictate the first sentence again, but this time pause between each word. (Notice when you say • **SCRATCH THAT**, only one word or section will be erased).

6. Say • **SELECT ALL,** • **DELETE SELECTION**

7. Say • **UNDO THAT**

8. Say • **SELECT Speech recognition through imagined.** • **DELETE SELECTION**

9. Say • **INSERT BEFORE** I know (*This should move the cursor to the location before the sentence I know I must create...)*

10. Now dictate: **This will help me get my work done faster.**

11. Say • **INSERT AFTER** create a

12. Say •**speech** to add the word speech <u>after</u> create a...and <u>before</u> the word profile.

Repeat this exercise to get practice using these quick correct commands.

6.2 Correcting with Recognition Window

In Lesson 5, you practiced using the **SELECT and SAY** method to correct. Often Dragon Dictate would recognize your incorrect word or phrase when you repeated it. If the word or phrase was still incorrect, you were told to use the keyboard to make the correction. This does make the correction in your document but doesn't really help Dragon Dictate learn your unique speech.

The **Recognition Window** is a built-in tool that allows you to **correct** and **train** mistakes to help Dragon Dictate improve its accuracy. Some people find using the Recognition Window feature to be tricky at first. However, learning to use the Recognition Window feature can be beneficial because you are not just correcting your mistakes but you are also training Dragon Dictate to recognize your speech and the kinds of things you say to improve your individual profile.

When you correct words with the •**CORRECT** command, the Recognition Window will appear with **alternative interpretations** of the word or phrase. The first alternative is the interpretation that Dragon Dictate entered in the document. The additional alternatives are the top suggestions Dragon Dictate is giving for the correction. Most of the time the correct word or phrase will be listed as one of these alternatives.

6.3 Using the CORRECT command vs. SELECT and SAY

- Open a New Notepad and **dictate** the following sentence **pausing** as indicated after each phrase.

  The two employees (*pause*) **went to the** (*pause*) **office to** (*pause*) **many times.**

- Say **CORRECT to** (*Notice the **Recognition Window** will appear with alternative choices*)

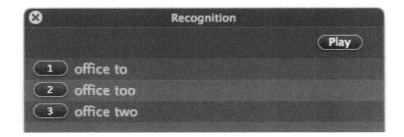

- Say •**PICK or CHOOSE 2** or whatever number may be correct. (*Notice choosing correct alternative automatically replaces the incorrect text and closes the recognition window*)

  The two employees went to the office too many times.

- Now dictate the following sentence again, this time **without** pausing.

The two employees went to the office too many times.

- Say •**CORRECT to** and you will notice that the entire sentence will probably be selected this time. (The Recognition Window operates on dictated utterances. Dragon Dictate has its own ideas about what constitutes an utterance, based partly on where you pause when dictating. Therefore, extra words may appear in the recognition window. The Correct feature still works the same).

The two employees went to the office too many times.

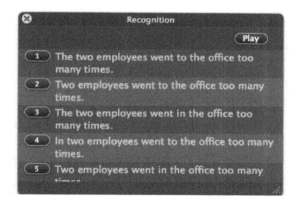

- Say •**Cancel Recognition** (*This will close the recognition window without making any changes*)

- Say •**Select All** and **Delete Selection** to clear your Note Pad screen.

When you correct words using the •**CORRECT** command, Dragon Dictate stores this correction and the probability of missing the same word again in the same context diminishes drastically. This is how people can move from a respectable 92-96% accuracy to a superb 97-100 percent accuracy on familiar trained text.

Remember to follow these steps to correct with the recognition window:

1. Use the •**CORRECT** *<some word>* or **<some word through some word>** to choose misrecognitions.

2. If a correct alternative is showing in the recognition window**,** say **Choose** or **Pick** <number> of the correct alternative (*you can also click the numbered button at the left with your mouse instead of using your voice*).

3. If the correct alternative does not appear in the recognition window list, say **Cancel Recognition** (*This will close the recognition window without making any changes*)

4. Use the **SELECT and SAY** command or use your **keyboard** to make additional corrections.

6.4 More Practice Dictating and Correcting

1. Open a New Notepad and dictate the following sentences saying **NEW PARAGRAPH** at the end of each sentence. (Be sure to dictate the ending punctuation marks.)

   The two employees went to the office too many times.

   Once upon a time, in a land far, far away, there lived a green giant.

   Once again, in the heat of the night, the fish were biting.

   As the saying goes, by the light of the moon, it happened one night.

   Over and over again, between the lines, it was often said.

   When in doubt, discuss the options and plan accordingly.

   He wants to go to the Olympics once in his life.

   Mr. Wright will write the right instructions on the assignment.

   They're on their way there.

   To improve your accuracy, always correct every mistake you make.

   Don't leave errors up in the air!

   Can I advise you on the advice you are giving to others?

   I don't know whether you have noticed, but the weather is awful today!

   He threw the ball through the target.

   Live the life you imagined.

   Two wrongs don't make a right.

   What goes up must come down.

   It does not matter who you are or where you come from; the ability to triumph begins with you.

   If you care at all, you'll get some results. If you care enough, you'll get incredible results.

   Our greatest glory is not in never falling, but in getting up every time we do.

   Even if you are on the right track, you'll get run over if you just sit there.

2. Proofread and make all corrections using the **CORRECT** command. (Remember you can correct using the **Select and Say** feature or by using the keyboard if the incorrect words still do not appear).

3. Say • **FILE, CLOSE**

4. Say • **PRESS SAVE**, name document "**Practice Sentences**"

5. To Print Say •**SHOW PRINT** and Say •**PRESS PRINT** *(or you can choose and click print by hand)*

6.5 Proofreading

Proofreading is the process of carefully reviewing text for errors, especially surface errors such as spelling, punctuation, grammar and extra or omitted words. Proofreading is the most crucial step you need to complete any time you are preparing documents.

Speech recognition errors can be different than typing errors. For example, Dragon Dictate will never misspell a word. However, it may misrecognize what you say and type the incorrect word or include extra words.

Dragon Dictate can read text back to you. Hearing your text can help you catch mistakes, especially ones that a spelling or grammar checker might miss. Dragon Dictate includes a text-to-speech feature that allows your text to be read in a synthesized voice. This is very beneficial for proofreading your documents because it allows you to listen to the flow of your writing, so you can decide where to make changes during editing. It can also help in verifying word pronunciations.

What You Say	Will do This
Read or **Proofread** (the word(s)) "text" [through| "text"]	Reads out loud the specified text.
Read or **Proofread the Selection**	Reads out loud the selected text.
Read or **Proofread (the) Document**	Reads out loud the current document.

Tip: Be sure your speakers or headset is properly configured to hear text-to-speech. You can also change the text-to-speech voice features by going to System Preferences, Speech.

Dictate the following paragraph including punctuation marks: (Do not correct any mistakes)

Training is essential for successful use of speech recognition software. An individual must learn to adjust the microphone properly, create a speech profile, and learn how to speak clearly to the computer to optimize recognition. The user must also learn the operational procedures of the software. Most individuals are surprised at how fast and how accurately they can type by voice after only a few hours of practice.

1. Say •**READ THE DOCUMENT**

2. Say •**READ Training through software** (*This should read the first sentence*)

3. Say •**SELECT create a speech profile**

4. Say •**READ THE SELECTION**

Select different sections of this paragraph and experiment with the **READ THE SELECTION**. (These will be useful commands when proofreading in the future).

LESSON 7—Reinforcing Dictation Skills & Evaluating Progress

7.1 Dictating Numbers and Symbols

Numbers and symbols are also easy to dictate. In most cases, you can dictate them the same way you would normally say them. Dates, phone numbers, currency, zip codes and times of day will often appear in the correct format if you dictate them without pausing.

Tips for dictating numbers:

To enter	Say
4	"four" or "numeral four"
23	"twenty three"
179	"one hundred seventy nine," "one hundred and seventy nine," *or* "one seventy nine"
5,423	"five comma thousand four twenty three"
142,015	"one hundred forty two thousand and fifteen"
127,400,042	"one hundred twenty seven million four-hundred thousand forty-two"
$45	"forty five dollars"
$99.50	"ninety nine dollars and fifty cents"
8:30 p.m.	"eight thirty pm"
May 15, 2003	"May fifteen comma two thousand three" (note: saying "comma" is optional)
Oakland, CA 99077	"Oakland California 99077"

Here is a list of some popular symbols:

'	• APOSTROPHE	©	• COPYRIGHT SIGN
's	• APOSTROPHE S	™	• TRADEMARK SIGN
\	• BACK SLASH	®	• REGISTERED SIGN
[	• OPEN BRACKET	#	• NUMBER SIGN
	• CLOSE BRACKET	%	• PERCENT SIGN
"	• OPEN QUOTE	<	• OPEN ANGLE BRACKET
"	• CLOSE QUOTE	<	• LESS THAN SIGN
—	• DASH	>	• CLOSE ANGLE
...	• ELLIPSIS	>	• GREATER THAN SIGN
(	• OPEN PAREN	&	• AMPERSAND
)	• CLOSE PAREN	—	• UNDERSCORE
~	• TILDE (til-dah)			• VERTICAL BAR
@	• AT SIGN	+	• PLUS SIGN
~	• EURO SIGN	=	• EQUALS SIGN
!	• EXCLAMATION MARK	?	• QUESTION MARK
$	• DOLLAR SIGN	-	• MINUS SIGN

Create a **New Note Pad** and practice dictating the numbers and symbols in these charts. Again, don't worry if Dragon Dictate does not recognize all of these. You will learn how to **TRAIN** them later.

7.2 Dictating Numbers

Practice dictating numbers. You can dictate the following across the screen by saying "**tab key**" after each entry or you can list them underneath each other by saying "**enter**".
*Remember, you can use the **Select** or **Correct** command and **choose** corrections from the correction list for numbers also.

Numbers:

| 12 | 35 | 60 | 125 | 750 | 3143 | 5,185,000 | 3 (numeral 3) |

Currency:

Dictate the following currency by saying (_____dollars and ____ cents) Example: (Seven dollars and 75 cents *will show* $7.75)

$5.15 [Tab key] $123.25 $1366 $1,350,000

Dates:

Dictate the following dates. Just say month, day, year together and you will not need to say the comma. To dictate the numeric form say "slash" for the /.

February 14, 1996   2/14/1996
May 16, 2001   5/16/2001
August 21, 2010   8/24/2010

Times:

Dictate the following times by saying the time along with AM or PM: (Don't worry if the format is not identical).

1:30 PM   5:15 PM   10:10 PM   6:20AM   3:45 AM

Phone Numbers:

Dictate the following phone numbers without saying the hyphens: (Don't hesitate between the numbers)

472-4564   602-334-5678
555-1212   309-682-0544
480-472-0395   1-800-749-1844

ZIP Codes:

Dictate the following zip codes. Say the city, full state name, and zip together--you do not need to say "comma". Dragon will change the state to a two letter abbreviation.

61615   89121   Mesa, AZ 85205   Boston, MA 02460

SAVE your document: with the name "**Dictating Numbers**"

To Print Say •**SHOW PRINT** and Say •**PRESS PRINT** (*or you can choose and click print by hand*)

7.3   More Dictating Practice

The following sentences combine words, numbers, symbols and punctuation marks. (You may need to refer to the special characters chart on the previous page and review dictation tips for dictating numbers.) Remember to dictate the entire sentences, do not try to correct as you dictate. Numbers and symbols can be awkward to dictate at first, so be patient.

Tammy paid $4.25 for paper, pencils, and pens.

My birthday is November 10.

"I am freezing," she said. "It is only 37° in here!"

Today's date is (*say today's month date and year*)**.**

I earned $25.50 for babysitting last night.

School starts at 8:05 AM and ends at 2:55 PM each day.

They have 35 horses, 20 fish, 5 cats, 7 birds and 2 hamsters.

Her address is 525 E. Brown, Atlanta, GA 78235.

His phone number is 888-352-1761.

Coca-Cola™

*Required fields

30*5 = 150

360/12 = 30

©2009   (Hint: *say copyright sign no space* 2009)

$32,865.25

35%

[Johnson & Johnson...]

500 >300 (*be sure to say greater than sign or it may write out greater than*)

725 < 837

250+25 -100 = 175

- **Proofread** and **correct** all the above sentences and phrases using the **CORRECT** and/or **SELECT and SAY** Commands.

- **SAVE** the document with the file name "More Dictating Practice"

- To Print Say •**SHOW PRINT** and Say •**PRESS PRINT** (*or you can choose and click print by hand*)

7.4   Comparing Voice and Keyboard

When people are first learning speech recognition software they often wonder how their productivity compares to using the keyboard and mouse.   Most people find that they can voice at least three times faster than they can type. However, some find that their beginning voice accuracy is lower when compared to their keyboarding results.

Take a one-minute timing on the following paragraphs by voice. Keep your eyes on the text and do not look at the screen as you read. Do not stop at the end of a line but just keep reading through the entire paragraph. Do NOT stop or correct any errors. When the minute is up turn off your microphone.

Press the enter key four times to leave space and then take a one-minute timing on the same paragraphs by using the **keyboard**. Keep your eyes on the text and do not look at the screen as you type. Do NOT backspace or correct any errors. (You will determine your speed and accuracy following the directions on the next page).

	wpm
(*Tab key*) **Credit cards can make shopping very convenient, and they**	12
can help you keep track of the money you spend. Some items	24
such as renting a car or staying in a hotel may require a	36
customer to use a credit card. However, many card companies	48
and banks charge high fees for using their credit cards. (*NEW LINE*)	60
(*Tab key*)**You must realize that it may be better to pay in cash**	70
and not use a credit card. If you apply for a credit card,	82
you should shop for the best credit terms. Some card	93
companies do not charge yearly fees. Some may offer you	104
benefits such as extended warranties or money back on the	116
merchandise you buy with their credit cards. Read the fine	128
print and evaluate all the information. You may be surprised	140
at the differences between the terms of various credit cards. (*NEW LINE*)	152
(*Tab key*)**Some credit cards are now being marketed to children.**	163
Parents now can obtain a credit card that is intended for	175
children as young as six years old. There is a transaction	187
fee every time the card is used. In addition, there is a	199
yearly fee and an additional fee each time the card is used.	211

|1 |2 |3 |4 |5 |6 |7 |8 |9 |10 |11   12

- Use your voice or keyboard to save this document as "**Evaluating Progress**". Keep document open for following lesson.

7.5 Evaluating Progress

In traditional keyboarding classes, teachers normally count every five characters as a word. This formula makes evaluating typing ability consistent from typist to typist. The formula counts spaces.

Voice or keyboard the answers to the following questions, below the timings you took.

First, determine your words per minute for both your voice and keyboard timings. Do this by looking at the number next to the last complete line. For any partial lines, you can determine how many words to add by looking at the number listed at the bottom of the timing.

1. What are your words per minute by **voice**?

2. What are your words per minute by **keyboard**?

3. How much faster did you voice the timing vs. keyboard the timing?

Second, proofread and **bold** or <u>underline</u> all of the errors in each of the timings. To determine your overall accuracy %, take your words per minute and subtract the total errors and then divide by your total words per minute.

4. How many errors did you have in the voiced timing?

5. How many errors did you have in the keyboard timing?

6. Which method had better accuracy?

- **SAVE** your **Evaluating Progress** document again to update changes and **PRINT**.

Chances are, based on the keyboarding formula; you are already speaking 110-140 words per minute or even faster! Anything over 100 wpm is great. Remember accuracy is more important than speed. Trying to talk faster will only cause more errors. Speaking in your natural voice is the key!

After completing these lessons, you should find that your accuracy level is somewhere around 95%. If it is lower, you should do additional voice training by following the steps for **4.6 Voice Training to Improve Accuracy** back on pages 26-27.

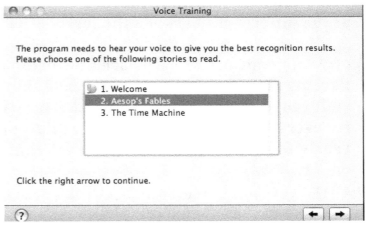

LESSON 8—Enhancing Your Speech Profile

Lessons 1-7 were designed to teach the basics of using Dragon Dictate. Learning how to create a profile, check your microphone, conduct voice training, and use the basic dictation tips and commands are the beginning steps in using speech recognition efficiently.

Being able to dictate at over 100 wpm with 95% or better accuracy is often sufficient enough for the casual speech recognition user. However, most people that use speech recognition as a daily tool expect to achieve a 98% or better accuracy level.

Lessons 8- 12 will help you increase your overall accuracy and productivity by learning many additional Dragon Dictate features including:

- **Using the Vocabulary Editor**

- **Adding and Training Words**

- **Customizing your Vocabulary**

- **Using Additional Commands**

- **Creating Custom Commands**

- **Using Text Edit and other applications**

- **Applying Dictation, Correction and Formatting Concepts**

- **Using Spelling and Commands Modes**

- **Navigating documents**

- **Conducting Web navigation/searches**

- **Preparing e-**

- **Creating Letters and Reports**

- **Taking Notes**

Remember, speech recognition is a skill and all skills take practice. Don't expect perfection. Be patient and work through these lessons step-by-step and you will continue to see improvements as you enhance your overall speech profile.

8.1 Vocabulary Editor

One of the most important features in Dragon Dictate is the Vocabulary Editor. The Vocabulary Editor Window is the user interface for viewing and editing the list of words, phrases, and symbols that Dragon Dictate can type for you in dictation mode.

- Say **Bring Dictate to Front** or click icon Status Window icon to activate Dragon Dictate bar.

- Say **SHOW VOCABUALRY EDITOR** or click on the Tools menu and choose Vocabulary Editor.

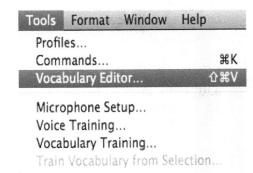

(There will be a brief delay the first time you open the vocabulary editor window while Dragon Dictate generates a built-in list of over 150,000 words. After the first use, this window will open quickly).

The **Vocabulary Editor** is a list of **ALL** the words in the Dragon Dictate dictionary. You can also just view the words that are already **Built-in** or specific to the **User**.

Notice words are listed alphabetically. To find a word quickly, you can start typing the word and press enter.

- Type super and press enter. Notice when you scroll the word supercalifragilisticexpialidocious comes up because it is already in the Dragon dictionary. You can train this word by clicking on

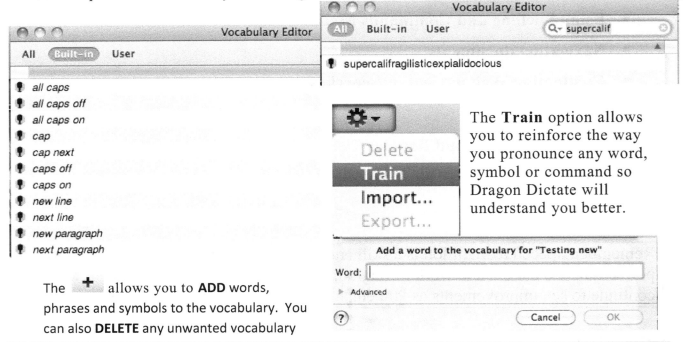

The **Train** option allows you to reinforce the way you pronounce any word, symbol or command so Dragon Dictate will understand you better.

The ➕ allows you to **ADD** words, phrases and symbols to the vocabulary. You can also **DELETE** any unwanted vocabulary

8.2 Add and Train Words

If you have troublesome words or unique names that you are going to use over and over again, it is best to add and train them using the Vocabulary Editor. Unique words, names and phrases can easily be added by using the following steps:

A. Say • **Show Vocabulary Editor,** click the ➕ icon to **Add** a word or phrase.

B. Type the word or phrase to be added.

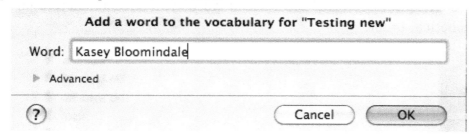

C. Click the Advanced arrow to expand window choices. (*If a word sounds different than it is spelled you can key how it sounds under spoken form otherwise leave it blank*)

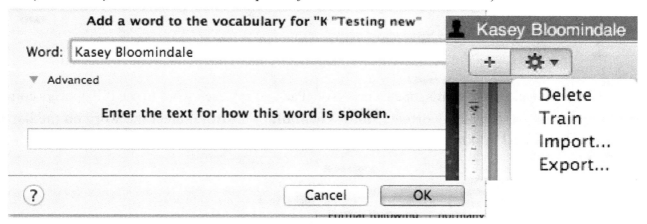

D. Click **OK** and with the word selected choose **Train** to dictate your pronunciation of the word 3 times.

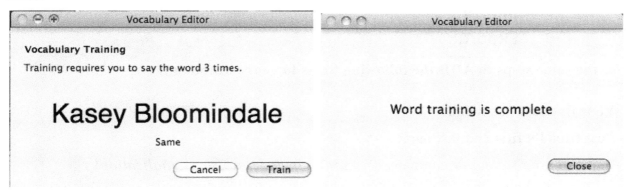

E. Click **Close**

Follow the steps in A-E to add the following words:

--Kasey Bloomindale (*notice no "g"*)

--Wowzer

--bibbidybobbidyboo

--oinkers

- If you click on the **User** option, you will see a list of words you have added to your vocabulary in alphabetical order.

- After you add these words, open a new Note Pad and say each word to see if it appears correctly.
- If any of these are not correct, **Show Vocabulary Editor**, select the word on the list and choose **TRAIN** to retrain the pronunciation.

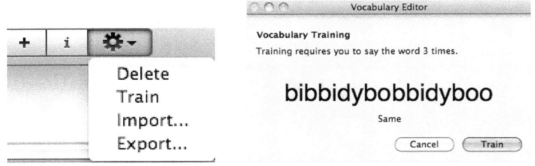

Use the same steps to ADD the following items to your vocabulary:

--Your first and last name

--Best friend's first and last name

--Name of your school or company (*be sure to include proper capitalization*)

Follow the steps on the next page to learn more about adding a word that has an abbreviation or sounds different than it is spelled.

8.3 Adding Words with Spoken Form

- Say • **Show Vocabulary Editor,** click the ✚ icon to **Add** a word or phrase. (Be sure the full screen is showing by clicking the Advanced downlist arrow).

Notice you can add a spoken form for any word or phrase. This is helpful for businesses and organizations that have their own specific terms and unique words or abbreviations. Basically, you are training the computer to type a specific Word or Phrase when you say the unique trained pronunciation.

In this example, you are adding the word Skyline High School by saying SHS. Notice the **Pronunciation**: SHS is listed under the written text in the training window.

- Type **Skyline High School** after Word and type **SHS** for how this word is spoken and click **Train.**

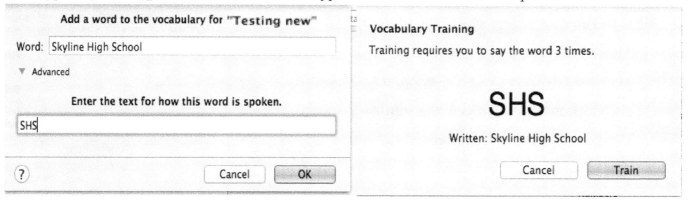

- To **Train** you will say the **Prounciation SHS** three times.. **NOT** the written word Skyline High School. Click Close when the Word training is complete.

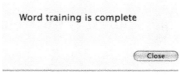

To see the added word in Vocabulary Editor, click on the **User** tab. Notice Skyline High School is added to the vocabulary list not SHS. However, if you select Skyline High School and choose Train the training window indicates the pronunciation SHS.

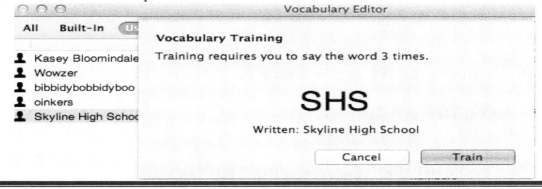

8.4 Practice Adding Words to Your Vocabulary and Dictating Sentences

--Use the steps you just learned in 8.3 to add the following written words with spoken forms to your vocabulary.

Written Form (WORD)	Spoken Form (PRONUNCIATION)
Lowell Junior High School	**LJHS**
Future Business Leaders of America	**FBLA**
email@yahoo.com **(use your e-mail)**	**work e-mail**
Johnson & Johnson Law Office	**J and J**

--Dictate the following sentences using Text Edit instead of the Dragon Note Pad. (Say **New Paragraph** to leave a blank line between each sentence).

- Say • **OPEN TEXT EDIT**

    My name is (*your name*).

    My best friend is (*friend's first and last name*).

    Kasey Bloomindale has a dog named Wowzer.

    The pigs were called oinkers in the story.

    Cinderella's fairy godmother chanted bibbidybobbidyboo.

    I go to school (*or work*) **at** (*name of your school or company name*).

    My sister goes to SHS (*computer will spell out Skyline High School*).

    The FBLA club is selling candy to go to California. (*computer will spell out Future Business Leaders…*)

    My e-mail address is work e-mail (*computer will write your e-mail address*).

    My dad works at J and J (*computer will write Johnson & Johnson Law Office*).

- Select and proofread each sentence. Practice using the **"READ THE SELECTION"** command from page 40.

- Make all corrections using the **CORRECT** or **SELECT and SAY** commands.

- Reinforce the pronunciation of any words that did not appear correctly by saying • **SHOW VOCABULARY EDITOR,** type the word in the search box and then choose **TRAIN**.

- Say •**SAVE THE DOCUMENT,** •**Press SAVE,** and name the document **Vocabulary Practice Sentences.**

- To Print Say •**SHOW PRINT** and Say •**PRESS PRINT** (*or you can choose and click print by hand*)

Besides correcting words or phrases using the recognition window and adding and training words using the Vocabulary Editor. Dragon Dictate has other tools that will help you customize your vocabulary, add and train words quickly, and make custom commands and shortcuts.

8.5 Customizing Your Vocabulary

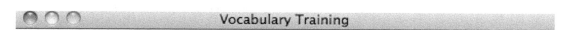

Tools	Format	Window	Help

Profiles...
Commands...   ⌘K
Vocabulary Editor...   ⇧⌘V

Microphone Setup...
Voice Training...
Vocabulary Training...
Train Vocabulary from Selection...

Vocabulary Training—is a quick way to have Dragon analyzes your chosen documents to add any unrecognized words to your vocabulary all at once. Following are the steps you would take to analyze specific documents and add any unrecognized words to your vocabulary all at once.

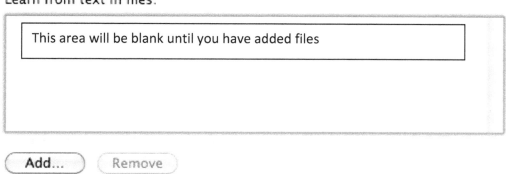

● ○ ○   Vocabulary Training

Dragon Dictate can analyze documents to determine your writing style. This improves accuracy by helping Dragon Dictate learn about the way you put words together. For this reason, it is important that Dragon Dictate analyzes documents written by you, not someone else.

To have Dragon Dictate analyze documents click the "Add..." button in below and choose documents from the Open File Dialog Box. You can also drag files directly into this window.

Learn from text in files:

This area will be blank until you have added files

(Add...)   (Remove)

After clicking **ADD**, navigate to the location of the file(s) you would like to have analyzed. The example below shows a list of files in a folder called Medical Cases. You would select the file(s) you want analyzed and click **OPEN**.

When you click **Open** all of the files will appear in the **Learn from text in files** box. If you changed your mind, you can select and **remove** any unwanted file.

Click the next arrow. (All documents listed will be analyzed for words that are not in your vocabulary)

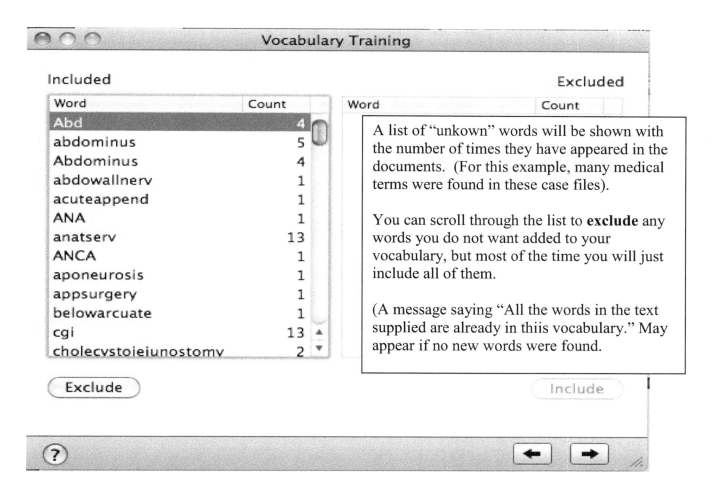

A list of "unkown" words will be shown with the number of times they have appeared in the documents. (For this example, many medical terms were found in these case files).

You can scroll through the list to **exclude** any words you do not want added to your vocabulary, but most of the time you will just include all of them.

(A message saying "All the words in the text supplied are already in thiis vocabulary." May appear if no new words were found.

Click the next arrow (The following messages will appear).

Vocabulary Training is being processed.

Processing...

Vocabulary Training is complete.

You may return to Vocabulary Training and add more samples to improve Dragon Dictate's ability to recognize your voice. To return to Vocabulary Training, select "Vocabulary Training..." from the "Tools" menu.

Follow these steps to have Dragon analyze any of your documents to add words to your vocabulary.

8.6 Create Your Own Word List

You can also prepare a list of your own unique words to add. The list can be made in Dragon Note Pad or any word processing program that can save as a .txt document.

- **Open** a **New Notepad** to create your own unique word list.

- Start with these unique movie words and add at least 5 more of your own. (Suggestions may include school organizations, clubs, first & last name of friends or any special terms you may use).

- Choose **File**, **SAVE AS** name file **My list** and be sure to choose the File Format **Plain text document**.

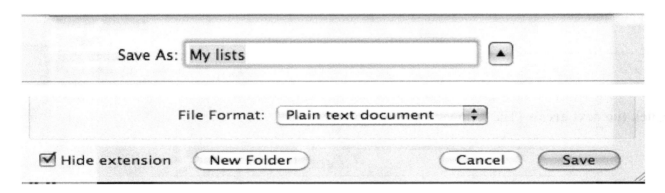

8.7 Use Vocabulary Training to Add Word List to Vocabulary

Follow the Steps to have Dragon analyze your My List file.

- Say •SHOW VOCABULARY TRAINING

Learn from text in files:

My Files.txt

- Drag your **My list.txt** file to the **Learn from text files** box **OR** click add and browse to the My List file and click **OPEN**.

- **Click** the **next arrow**.

Add...   Remove

- Notice the new words that have been found are listed in the included area. (If a word doesn't appear then it is already in your Dragon vocabulary....for this example notice Sweet and Jiminy Cricket did not appear).

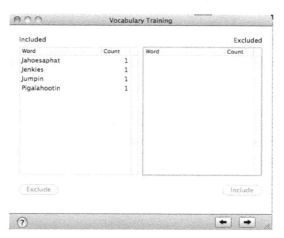

- **Click** the **next arrow** to complete the vocabulary training steps.

- You will see the messages **Vocabulary is processing** and **Vocabulary Training is complete.**

- **Click Done**

8.8 Use Vocabulary Editor to Review and Train Words

When new words have been added to your vocabulary, they may or may not appear correctly the first time you dictate them. This is because Dragon Dictate may need to hear your unique pronunciation of the word. (Remember, you can pronounce words by **training** the word in the **vocabulary editor**).

Check the words you just added:

- Open Text Edit

- **Dictate** all the words you added in your My List document to determine if they need to be trained.

Sweet Jenkies
Jumpin
Jahoesaphat
Pigalahootin
Jiminy Cricket

- Say **Quit Text Edit, Press Don't Save**

- Say **Vocabulary Editor**, choose User option and **Train** any words that did not appear correctly. (See Lesson 8.2 pages 49-50 to review how to Train words.)

8.9 Creating Custom Commands (MACROS)

You can easily create your own commands or shortcuts to save you time as you dictate. These voice commands are popular for addresses, signature blocks, and sections of text that are often repeated.

- Say • **Bring Dictate to Front** or click on Dragon Dictate button

- Say: • **SHOW COMMANDS** (Or click Tools, Commands on the DragonBar). This will bring up the Commands window.

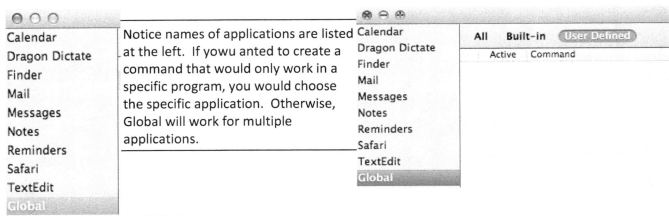

- Choose the User Defined option

- Choose File, New Command from the Dragon Bar or click the second + sign at the bottom of the window to add a new command

- Notice a new command name option will appear with choices to the right.

- The **Command Name** box is where you need to name your Text Macro with at <u>least</u> two words. Some people like to use the word insert as part of the command name. Examples: Insert My Address or Insert Signature Block. Using the word "insert" as part of the Command Name avoids naming it something that you may want to dictate as text later. However, the word insert is not required.

- The **Command Description** box is *optional* but can be used if you think it would be helpful in identifying the content for the Command Name.

- The **Content** list allows you to choose the program application for the command. It is suggested that this always be set to **Global**.

- For creating Text Macros, the **Type** should always be set to **Text Macro**.

8.10 Practice Creating Your Own Custom Commands (MACROS)

- Be sure a **New Command Window** is showing on your screen. If not, choose File, New Command from the Dragon Bar or click the 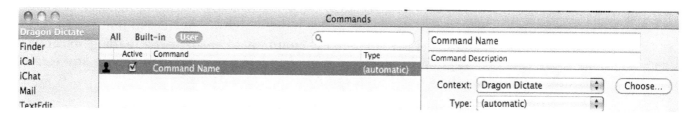 at the bottom of the window to add a new command.

- For the **Command Name**, type or dictate: **Insert Speaking Solutions Address**
- For the **Description**, type or dictate: **Company Address**
- Choose **Global** for **content** and **Text Macro** for **Type**.
- In the **text** section, type or dictate the following:

Speaking Solutions, Inc.

2445 Lake Shore Drive

Union, NE 68455

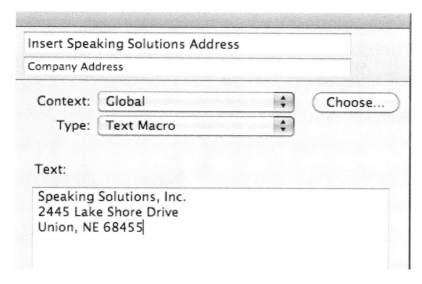

*(Keep in mind that you can also **copy** and **paste** text from other applications into the text area if it is easier.)*

- Click the **SAVE** button at the bottom of the Commands window to save the command with specified text.
- Follow these same steps to add more custom commands.

8.11 Use Copy and Paste to Create Custom Commands

- Open Text Edit

- **Dictate** the following Preamble (don't forget to dictate all punctuation.)

  We the people of the United States, in order to form a more perfect union, establish justice, insure domestic tranquility, provide for the common defense, promote the general welfare, and secure the blessings of liberty to ourselves and our posterity, do ordain and establish this Constitution for the United States of America. (New Paragraph)

- Proofread and correct any errors.

- Be sure the Dictate menu is showing--Say **SELECT ALL, COPY THE SELECTION**

- Say: • SHOW COMMANDS (Or click Tools, Commands on the DragonBar).

- Add new command:
    - For the **Command Name**, type or dictate: **Insert Preamble**
    - Choose **Global** for **content** and **Text Macro** for **Type**.
    - In the **text** section, Say **PASTE FROM CLIPBOARD**: (This should copy the preamble paragraph you dictated.)

- Practice creating your own custom commands/shortcuts…home address, signature block, school or company address, etc… Be sure your content is always set to **Global** and Type is **Text Macro**. Remember, you can even copy text that is already in other documents or on a website and turn it into a custom command vs. dictating from scratch)

8.12   Test Your Custom Commands (MACROS)

- **OPEN TEXT EDIT**
- Say **each** of the commands you added (The full text should appear if it doesn't. Try repeating the command)
    - Insert Speaking Solutions Address
    - Insert Preamble
    - Insert home address
    - Insert signature block
    - ANY OTHER COMMANDS YOU ADDED

The following page explains how you can view, edit and delete custom commands.

8.13 Viewing and Editing Custom Commands

Commands may be **edited** — modified, created, activated and deactivated, and deleted — in the Commands Window.

- To **open the Commands window**:
  - Choose Tools > Commands.
  - Choose File > New Command. This is the same as choosing Tools > Commands and then pressing the button to create a new command.

- To **switch among command lists**:
  - In the left column, select a command set — Global, or an application context.
  - At the top of the middle column, click All, Built-in, or User Defined.
  - It is the combination of both these settings that determines which commands are displayed.

- To **activate or deactivate a command**:
  - Click the checkbox to the left of the command's name.
  - A deactivated command still exists, but it is not listed in the available commands window. You cannot issue the command, and Dragon Dictate doesn't have to consider that phrase as a possible command when you say it. So, deactivating unused commands can be useful; but you probably should wait, before doing so, to see which commands you really don't need.

- To **delete a command**:
  - Select the command, and press Delete, or choose Delete from the tool (gear) menu.
  - You can't delete an unmodified built-in command. Deleting a built-in command that you've

- To **edit a command**:
  - Select the command name
  - The current content will show in the right column and any of these details can be changed.
  - Click **Save** at the bottom of the command window to update any changes.

Note: The changes that you make in the Commands window might not be registered until you close the Commands window.

LESSON 9—Using Commands

Remember the difference between <u>dictating</u> and giving a <u>command</u>. **Dictating** is when you want the computer to type what you say. A **command** is when you are telling the computer to perform a task.

When first learning speech recognition software it is important to learn the basics before trying to memorize a lot of commands. You should now have a good understanding of the dictation basics and how to improve your speech profile by adding, training, and correcting words.

Using speech recognition software doesn't mean that everything needs to be hands-free. However, as you become more familiar with Dragon features, you may find it beneficial to use more voice commands. Basic command tips with the most commonly used commands were introduced in Lesson 3.3 (see page 20). This lesson will focus on using more commands for navigating and formatting documents.

Again, don't try to memorize a lot of commands. You will learn what commands are more useful for you as you dictate and become more familiar with using Dragon Dictate with other programs. The voice commands will become a natural part of your dictation the more you use them.

9.1 Show Available Commands

The **Available Commands Window** is a window that list commands that can be used for whatever program you are using. A list of global commands appears if there is no list of specific commands available for a particular program. Many people find this command window very helpful, and others find it distracting. Just like using the task pane in other programs, it is a personal preference.

The Command Window can be open by choosing "**Show Available Commands**" from the Window menu on the Dragon Dictate Bar or by saying "**SHOW AVAILABLE COMMANDS**". When this window opens it floats over the screen, so you can easily position it where it is easy to see.

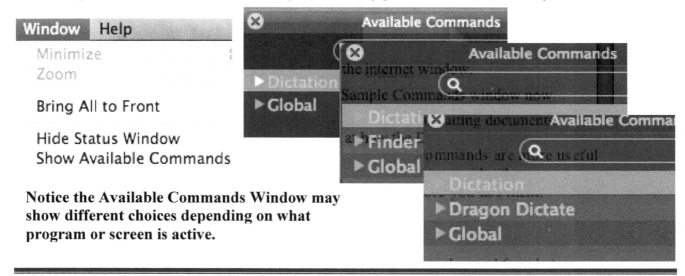

Notice the Available Commands Window may show different choices depending on what program or screen is active.

▪ Keep your **Microphone OFF** and choose "**Show Available Commands**" from the Window menu on the Dragon Dictate Bar.

> Take a few minutes to navigate through the command window choices. Notice there are numerous commands available under each category and there is often more than one command that will perform the same function. You will notice you have been using many of these commands in previous lessons.

> It is not necessary to memorize a lot of commands. However, it is important to understand what commands to use.

Dictation Commands are commands that you use on a daily basis to edit, proofread and format text and are only available in the Dictation Mode.

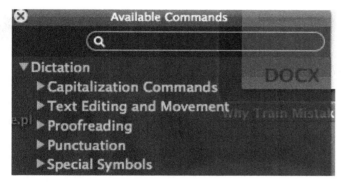

Global Commands are available in every **mode** except the sleep mode and are commands that control the computer as a whole such as opening and closing programs, pressing keyboard combinations and navigating with the mouse. This will also include commands you add.

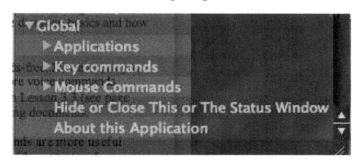

Application Commands usually open, activate, close, and quit programs.

Key Commands are used to voice keyboard combinations or short cuts that are helpful in situations where you might otherwise have to use the keyboard or when there is no built-in command that lets you say what you want done.

Mouse Commands are used to control the movement of the cursor.

9.2 Reviewing Basic Commands

The following list is a quick reference to commands that were introduced in Lessons 3-8. You may have already become comfortable using many of the basic commands.

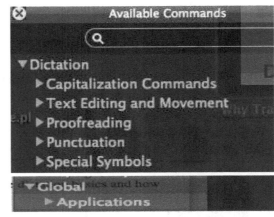

— **Basic Commands and Tips**—Lesson 3.3 Page 20

— **Capitalization commands**—Lesson 4.7 Page 49

— **Text Editing and Movement**—Lesson 4.3-4.4 Page 25-26

— **Proofreading**—Lesson 6.5 Page 40

— **Punctuation and Special Symbols**--Lessons 7.1 Page 41

— **Applications**—Lessons 3.3-3.5 on pages 21-22.

9.3 Practicing Application Commands

➢ **ACTIVATE, OPEN** or **SHOW** <name of application or feature> (Opens application or item)

➢ **HIDE** or **CLOSE** <name of application or feature> (Deactivates or hides a window item)

➢ **QUIT**<name of application or feature> (Deactivates and application)

➢ **SWITCH TO NEXT** OR **PREVIOUS APPLICATION** (toggles among open applications)

▪ Say • **OPEN MICROSOFT WORD**

▪ Say • **ACTIVATE MICROSOFT EXCEL**

▪ Say • **SWITCH TO PREVIOUS APPLICATION** (toggles among open applications)

▪ Say • **OPEN SAFARI (or browser of your choice)**

▪ Say • **SWITCH TO NEXT APPLICATION**

▪ Say • **QUIT MICROSOFT EXCEL**

▪ Say • **QUIT SAFARI**

▪ Say • **QUIT WORD**

▪ Say • **SHOW DATE AND TIME**

▪ Say • **HIDE APPLICATION**

▪ Say • **SHOW AVAILABLE COMMANDS**

▪ Say • **HIDE AVAILABLE COMMANDS**

Commands can sometimes be tricky. Practice opening, closing and switching between programs of your choice. Remember, you can always use your keyboard or mouse if you have trouble with voice commands.

9.4 Practicing Formatting Commands (Bold, Underline and Italicize)

Remember it is important to dictate your entire text before trying to correct or format. However, you can use the **UNDO LAST ACTION**, **REDO LAST ACTION** and **SCRATCH THAT** commands to quickly correct a mistake. Review Lesson 6.1 **QUICK CORRECTION COMMANDS** on Page 36.

Open Text Edit and dictate the paragraph below without formatting. Follow instructions below the paragraph to practice applying commands.

Learning to format with your voice is easy. You just need to know the proper commands for what you want the computer to do. It is actually best to format your document after you dictate your text instead of trying to format as you are dictating.

To bold, italicize, or underline text after it has already been dictated, you can either select the text and say <Desired command and selection> such as • **SELECT** *word/phrase*, •**BOLD SELECTION,** or you can use a Natural Command such as •**BOLD** *word/phrase*, or •**ITALICIZE** *word/phrase*.

- Say •**SELECT** voice, • BOLD THE SELECTION (be sure to say THE)
- Say •**ITALICIZE** voice
- Say •**UNDERLINE** proper commands
- Say •**BOLD** Learning
- Say •**ITALICIZE** computer
- Say •**UNDERLINE** format (notice it underlines one of the occurrences of the word format).
- Say **SELECT AGAIN** and the next occurrence will be selected
- Say **UNDERLINE THE SELECTION**
- Say **SELECT AGAIN** or **SELECT PREVIOUS** to move to the final occurrence
- Say **UNDERLINE THE SELECTION**

The formatted paragraph should now look like this:

Learning to <u>format</u> with your *voice* is easy. You just need to know the <u>proper commands</u> for what you want the *computer* to do. It is actually best to <u>format</u> your document after you dictate your text instead of trying to <u>format</u> as you are dictating.

Say **SAVE DOCUMENT** AS name file "Formatting Practice" and **PRESS SAVE**

To **remove any formatting** feature select the word(s) that are formatted and repeat the command. (This is like using the toggle key).

- Say •**SELECT** Learning, •**BOLD THE SELECTION** (bold is removed)
- Say •**SELECT** proper commands •**UNDERLINE THE SELECTION** (underline is removed)
- Say •**SELECT** voice •**BOLD THE SELECTION** (removes bold but not italic)
- Say •**SELECT** voice •**ITALICIZE THE SELECTION** (removes italic)

9.5 Practicing Aligning Text (Left, Right and Center)

The •**ALIGN TEXT** command is used to align text to the left margin, center of the document or to the right margin. You can use the **ALIGN TEXT** as you dictate or by selecting text when editing and formatting.

Aligning Text while Dictating:

8   Say right-hand man
9   Say • **ALIGN TEXT RIGHT** *(notice text moves to right margin)*
10   Say •**NEW LINE** *(notice cursor will remain at the right margin)*
11   Say central station
12   Say •**CAPITALIZE central station**
13   Say •**ALIGN TEXT CENTER** *(notice text is centered)*
14   Say •**NEW LINE** *(notice cursor will remain at center)*
15   Say •Lefty Jones
16   Say •**ALIGN TEXT LEFT**

The results should look like this in your document:

right-hand man

Central Station

Lefty Jones

When you dictated the alignment commands, the next line stayed at the alignment you dictated until you said a new alignment command. You can also apply alignment commands to individual text passages by selecting the text and saying the command. This prevents you from having to change the alignment back and forth.

Aligning Text after Dictating:

17   Say right-hand man
18   Say •**NEW LINE**
19   Say central station
20   Say •**CAPITALIZE central station**
21   Say •**NEW LINE**
22   Say •Lefty Jones (notice all three lines are aligned left)
23   Say •**SELECT** right-hand man, **ALIGN TEXT RIGHT**
24   Say •**SELECT** central station
25   Say •**ALIGN TEXT CENTER**

Notice Lefty Jones stayed left aligned. Most people prefer to use the ALIGN TEXT commands after dictating vs. while dictating.

9.6 Using Text Edit Commands to Voice-Edit

There is a difference between *correcting misrecognitions* and *voice-editing*. When **voice-editing,** you will fix *your* mistakes. At times, every writer will stumble over their words, change their mind, or use the wrong words for the tone of a particular paragraph. These errors cannot be blamed on the software. Nevertheless, they need to be edited. Learning to edit with your voice can be a huge timesaver and can improve your writing.

Fortunately, when using speech recognition software, spelling errors will be minimal, even absent from your writing. Dragon may misrecognize what you are saying and type the wrong word, but it *will* be spelled correctly! As far as the use of homonyms, the speech software makes logical guesses based on the context of the words in the sentence.

However, for this context checking feature to work properly, you must practice speaking in complete sentences and phrases. Speaking in full, uninterrupted sentences and phrases helps the software guess which part of speech, which homonym, or which spelling of the word you need typed. Sometimes it makes a difference in where you pause when speaking.

Example Phrase: As you work for higher speed in keyboarding

If you pause after the word **higher** before saying **speed**, you may get the word **hire** instead of **higher** because hire is grammatically correct. If you say **higher speed** together without pausing between the words, the computer will not make this mistake. (Try this same sentence yourself).

9.7 Practice Voice-Editing Commands

Dictate the following paragraph and then follow the steps below to practice editing.

People have the ability to carry on conversations and tell stories. Almost everyone can relate a story and say something meaningful. And now they have the software to turn their speech into words.

Proofread and correct any errors. Then apply the following voice-editing commands:

1. Say • **INSERT BEFORE** *ability to carry.* Pause briefly and say: **special**
2. Say • **UNDERLINE** conversations
3. Say • **Delete** Almost
4. Say • **Capitalize Everyone**
5. Say • **INSERT AFTER** relate a story, Say *comma* **express a point of view** *comma*
6. Say • **SELECT** *speech into words.* Pause briefly and say: **most important thoughts into a written form**
7. Compare your paragraph to the one below.

1   2   3-4

People have the **special** ability to carry on <u>conversations</u> and tell stories. Everyone can

5

relate a story, **express a point of view,** and say something meaningful. And now they have

6

the software to turn their **most important thoughts into a written form.**

LESSON 10—Dictation, Correction & Formatting Concepts

In the previous chapters, you learned many of the speech recognition dictation basics, correction strategies and formatting commands. You will practice applying these concepts when creating the following documents. **Remember it takes time and practice!**

- Tune your microphone **SHOW MICROPHONE SETUP**

- Dictate the text of the document first and then edit and format the text.

- Don't watch the screen when you dictate.

- Turn off the Microphone when you are not dictating.

- Use the "**READ SELECTION**" to help you proofread.

- Use **SELECT and SAY** to make corrections by selecting an incorrect word or and repeating the correct word or phrase.

- Use the **CORRECT** command to make corrections using the recognition window choose list.

- Use the **VOCABULARY EDITOR** command to **add** a word to the vocabulary

- Use the **TRAIN WORD** to reinforce your pronunciation of a word

- Format documents as your final step.

Below are two examples of reports you will create in this lesson.

PREVENTING COMPUTER INJURIES

Your Name

October 3, 2008

For April, Miguel, and Maria, the pains of repetitive stress injury came early in life. (The names have been changed to protect privacy.) For this trio, symptoms began in their elementary typing classes. By the time they reached the required middle school typing class, their pains were getting worse.

A Growing Problem

Repetitive Stress Injury (also known as RSI) has become a major problem. Many professionals are now at risk for RSI. For example:

- An estimated 25% of computer users will suffer some form of RSI during their careers.

- Over 1,800,000 workers have some form of RSI.

- Approximately 600,000 employees miss some work as a result of RSI.

- Using a keyboard or mouse for more than four hours a day is considered a risk factor for RSI.

- Prevention programs could eliminate 460,000 injuries every year.

THE NATURE OF VOICE WRITING

©Speaking Solutions 2001

People have the ability to carry on conversations and tell stories. Almost everyone can relate to a story and say something meaningful. And now they have the software to turn their speech into writing.

Voice-writing requires practice and lots of it. People adjust the pace of their writing to the efficiency of their input tools. In centuries past, writers would saddle their thoughts and slow them down to a walk when crafting paragraphs with pen and ink. Eventually, writers learned to type and entered their thoughts into typing machines at a trot, or even a gallop, to the rhythmic tapping of their fingers across the keyboard. By comparison, voice-writers produce copy at a run. Learning to think, compose, speak clearly, and edit at the speed of speech takes effort and rehearsal.

10.1 Dictate and Edit Short Report "Why Train Mistakes"

Some people like to use more voice navigation and formatting commands as they become familiar with speech recognition software. For this lesson, you will practice dictating, correcting and formatting with your voice as you create the following short report. Remember, you can always use your mouse or keyboard if you have trouble with any of the voice commands.

1. Turn on your microphone and **OPEN, Text Edit.**

2. Start with a clear screen. Dictate these three paragraphs separating each one with the
    • NEW PARAGRAPH command.

    Sometimes words are misspoken. With speech software, you should train each and every mistake. Always train errors. When you fix each mistake in the proper way, Dragon Dictate remembers. This will improve your accuracy.

    You can train words or phrases. If the proper word appears in the correction list, simply choose the proper word. If the proper word does not appear in the correction list, you must spell the word. You may need to record a word or phrase that is giving you difficulty.

    Training mistakes is the most important thing you can do to improve your recognition accuracy. If you train mistakes in the way explained in this book, you will notice the improvement in accuracy each and every day.

3. Proofread carefully and correct each and every mistake in the three paragraphs above using the
    SELECT and SAY, or **CORRECT** command. You may want to review the proofreading tips in Lesson 6.5 on Page 40.

4. Say **• SAVE THE DOCUMENT** and name the document **Why Train Mistakes?**

10.2 Practice Navigating/Moving around Document

Make sure your document **"Why Train Mistakes"** is still open on your screen.

- Say**• GO TO THE BEGINNING** to move to the top of the document.

- Say**• GO TO THE END** to move to the bottom of the document.

- Say**• SELECT When through Way**

- Say**• UNSELECT THAT**

- Say**• INSERT BEFORE MISSPOKEN**

- Say**• INSERT AFTER REMEMBERS**

- Say**• GO TO THE BEGINNING**

Keep document open for 10.3

10.3 Insert and Capitalize Headings

- With the cursor at the beginning of the document, dictate **Why Train Mistakes? • NEW PARAGRAPH**

- Say**• INSERT BEFORE You can train** (*this will move the cursor to the beginning of the second paragraph*)

- *Dictate* **Correction list • NEW PARAGRAPH (***Choose the correct number if more than one is selected*)

- Say**• INSERT BEFORE Training mistakes** (*this will move the cursor to the beginning of the third paragraph*)

- *Dictate* **Improving accuracy• NEW PARAGRAPH**

- Say • **SELECT Why train mistakes**

- Say • **UPPERCASE THE SELECTION** to create a title with all capital letters

- Say • **SELECT Correction list**

- Say • **CAPITALIZE THE SELECTION** to capitalize this heading

- Say • **SELECT Improving Accuracy**

- Say • **CAPITALIZE THE SELECTION** to capitalize this heading

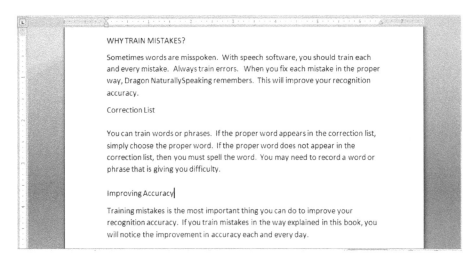

- Say • **SELECT ALL, READ THAT** (Listen as the computer reads your paragraphs)

- Proofread again and make all corrections

- Say •**Save the Document** (this will automatically save and update your "Why Train Mistakes" file you saved previously.)

- Say •**SHOW PRINT**, the print dialog box will appear, Say •**PRESS PRINT**

10.4 Dictate, Edit and Format Report "Preventing Computer Injuries"

1. Turn on your microphone and Say **OPEN TEXT EDIT**.

2. Dictate the following paragraph. Say • **OPEN PARENTHESES** for (Say • **CLOSE PARENTHESES** for). Fix all the errors at the end of the paragraph.

   For April, Miguel, and Maria, the pains of repetitive stress injury came early in life. (The names have been changed to protect privacy.) For this trio, symptoms began in their elementary typing classes. By the time they reached a required middle school typing class, their pains were getting worse.

   •NEW PARAGRAPH

3. To apply format commands, remember you can immediately SAY the command with the word THAT or THIS or SELECT the text and say <format command> THE SELECTION

4. Say • **GO TO BEGINNING** and add a title: Say • **preventing computer injuries**

   - **UPPERCASE THAT** or use **SELECT TEXT** and **SAY** • **UPPERCASE SELECTION**

   - **BOLD THAT**

   - **ITALICIZE THAT**

   - **UNDERLINE THAT**

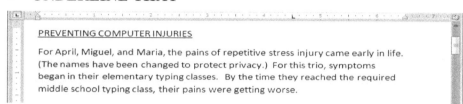

5. Say • **GO TO THE END** to move to the bottom of the document. Dictate the following paragraphs. (*When dictating the numbers with decimals, say **29 point 6** for 29.6*).

   Mayo Clinic study

   - **NEW PARAGRAPH**

   As people get older, a greater percentage of the population is impacted by repetitive stress injuries. In an interesting study at the Mayo Clinic in Scottsdale, Arizona, 29.6% of hospital respondents reported numbness, prickly sensations or abnormal sensitivity.

   - **NEW PARAGRAPH**

   Of the 257 respondents, 70 employees reported RSI related symptoms. Of those, 27 or 10.5% were classified with carpal tunnel syndrome, which is similar to that found in the general population in past studies.

6. Bold the **Mayo Clinic Study** subtitle saying:

   - **SELECT Mayo Clinic study**
   - **BOLD THE SELECTION**
   - **CAPITALIZE THIS**

---

7. Compare your document to the one below. Proofread and correct any mistakes using the **SELECT** and **SAY** or **CORRECT** commands. Remember, you can use the "**READ SELECTION**" commands to help you proofread. (See Lesson 6.5 on Page 40.)

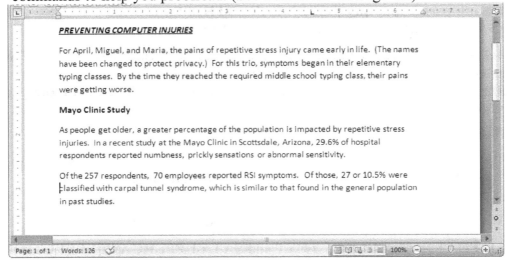

PREVENTING COMPUTER INJURIES

For April, Miguel, and Maria, the pains of repetitive stress injury came early in life. (The names have been changed to protect privacy.) For this trio, symptoms began in their elementary typing classes. By the time they reached the required middle school typing class, their pains were getting worse.

Mayo Clinic Study

As people get older, a greater percentage of the population is impacted by repetitive stress injuries. In a recent study at the Mayo Clinic in Scottsdale, Arizona, 29.6% of hospital respondents reported numbness, prickly sensations or abnormal sensitivity.

Of the 257 respondents, 70 employees reported RSI symptoms. Of those, 27 or 10.5% were classified with carpal tunnel syndrome, which is similar to that found in the general population in past studies.

8. Say • **SAVE THE DOCUMENT** and name the file **Preventing Computer Injuries**

10.5 Practice Inserting and Formatting Text

Make sure your Preventing Computer Injuries file is open.

1. Say • **GO TO THE END** to move to the end of the document.

2. Dictate the following. Use the • **NEW PARAGRAPH** command to separate the paragraphs/sections with a blank line. (*Say numbers normally such as **one million eight hundred thousand** for the number **1,800,000**)*

A Growing Problem

Repetitive stress injury (also known as RSI) has become a major problem. Many professionals are now at risk for RSI. For example:

An estimated 25% of computer users will suffer some form of RSI during their careers. Over 1,800,000 workers have some form of RSI.

Approximately 600,000 employees miss some work as a result of RSI.

Using a keyboard or mouse for more than four hours a day is considered a risk factor for RSI.

Prevention programs could eliminate 460,000 injuries every year.

3. Say **SELECT A Growing Problem** and say • **CAP THAT** • **BOLD THAT** • **ITALICIZE THAT** to format this subtitle.

4. Add to the Mayo Clinic Study heading...

   Say **INSERT AFTER Mayo Clinic Study** and say **on June 12, 2001 reported:**

5. Insert your name after the title. Say:

   INSERT AFTER *PREVENTING COMPUTER INJURIES*

   Say **•NEW PARAGRAPH** to leave a blank line.

   Dictate **Your Name.** (Note: Bold your name if it did not automatically bold.)

   Say **• NEW PARAGRAPH** (to leave a blank line)

6. Dictate **today's date**

7. Select these three lines and Say **•ALIGN THE TEXT CENTERED** (this should center your title, name and date)

8. Use your mouse to select the last four sentences and add bullets.

> Of the 257 respondents, 70 employees reported RSI symptoms. Of those, 27 or 10.5% were classified with carpal tunnel syndrome, which is similar to that found in the general population in past studies.
>
> **A Growing Problem**
>
> Repetitive Stress Injury (also known as RSI) has become a major problem. Many professionals are now at risk for RSI. For example:
>
> - An estimated 25% of computer users will suffer some form of RSI during their careers.
>
> - Over 1,800,000 workers have some form of RSI.
>
> - Approximately 600,000 employees miss some work as a result of RSI.
>
> - Using a keyboard or mouse for more than four hours a day is considered a risk factor for RSI.
>
> - Prevention programs could eliminate 460,000 injuries every year.

9. Proofread again and make all corrections.

10. Say **•SAVE THE DOCEMENT** (this will automatically save and update your "Why Train Mistakes" file you saved previously.)

11. Say **•SHOW PRINT**, the print dialog box will appear, Say **•PRESS PRINT**

10.6 Cut, Copy and Paste

COPY <WORD> or THE SELECTION – copies selected text

CUT <WORD> or THE SELECTION – cuts the selected text (removes it from the document)

PASTE IT HERE or PASTE FROM CLIPBOARD– inserts the copied or cut text into the document where cursor is.

1. Dictate the following passage and then follow the steps below to practice the cut, copy and paste commands above. Say **NEW LINE** after each sentence.

    You will soon be flying through your documents with voice commands making the necessary changes.
    Keep practicing!
    Do not be discouraged if you do not remember all the voice commands at first.
    Learning formatting commands takes time and practice.

2. Say **SELECT Keep practicing exclamation mark**, say **CUT THE SELECTION**

3. Say **GO TO THE BEGINNING** (moves cursor to beginning of first sentence), say **PASTE IT HERE**

4. Say **SELECT Learning THROUGH practice period**, say **CUT THE SELECTION**

5. Say **INSERT BEFORE You will**, say **PASTE IT HERE**

6. Say **SELECT Do not be THROUGH at first period**, say **CUT THE SELECTION**

7. Say **INSERT BEFORE You will**, say **PASTE IT HERE**

8. Say **SELECT Keep practicing exclamation mark**, say **COPY THE SELECTION**

9. Say **GO TO THE END**, say **PASTE IT HERE**

10. The final paragraph should read as follows:

    Keep practicing! Learning formatting commands takes time and practice. Do not be discouraged if you do not remember all the voice commands at first. You will soon be flying through your documents with voice commands making the necessary changes. Keep practicing!

11. Say •**SAVE THE DOCEMENT** (this will automatically save and update your "Preventing Computer Injuries" file you saved previously.)

12. Say •**SHOW PRINT**, the print dialog box will appear, Say •**PRESS PRINT**

10.7 Dictate, Edit and Format Report "The Nature of Voice-Writing"

1. Turn on your Microphone and **Say •OPEN TEXT EDIT** to create a new document.

2. Set your **Spacing** to **Double Spacing**. (You will need to say **New Line** at the end of each paragraph since you are on double spacing and Say **Tab Key** to indent paragraphs

3. Dictate the following report. (Remember to dictate all of the text without watching the screen. You will correct your errors and format text when you are done dictating.)

> **The Nature of Voice Writing** (*don't worry about the capitalization*)
> **NEW LINE**
> **Copyright sign, speaking solutions, 2010**
> **NEW LINE**
>   **People have the ability to carry on conversations and tell stories. Almost everyone can relate to a story and say something meaningful. And now they have the software to turn their speech into writing.**
>
>   **Voice-writing requires practice and lots of it. People adjust the pace of their writing to the efficiency of their input tools. In centuries past, writers would saddle their thoughts and slow them down to a walk when crafting paragraphs with pen and ink. Eventually, writers learned to type and entered their thoughts into typing machines at a trot, or even a gallop, to the rhythmic tapping of their fingers across the keyboard. By comparison, voice-writers produce copy at a run. Learning to think, compose, speak clearly, and edit at the speed of speech takes effort and rehearsal.**
>
>   **Inefficient keyboarding can retard the flow of ideas. It often causes writers, young writers in particular, to forget much of what they wish to communicate. Many potentially talented writers are intimidated or inhibited by their input tools. Inefficient typists, or those with poor penmanship, often shy away from the written craft. Poor scholars hesitate to write for fear that misspelled words will show them up.**
>
>   **But writing isn't spelling, typing, or penmanship. Writing is the artful communication of ideas in a written form. Speech recognition has made it possible for anyone who can think and speak clearly to write clearly as well. Inadequate spelling, erratic typing, or poor penmanship are no longer barriers to written expression. Writing can now become a process of thinking and expressing, supported by careful proofreading and thoughtful editing.**

4. Say •**SELECT The nature of voice-writing UPPERCASE THE SELECTION**

5. Say •**SELECT The Nature THROUGH 2010** (*this should select the first two lines*)

6. Say •**ALIGN THE TEXT CENTERED**

7. Proofread and compare your document to the sample on the next page and make any corrections

8. Say •**SAVE THE DOCEMENT** and name the file **Nature of Voice Writing**

9. Say •**SHOW PRINT**, the print dialog box will appear, Say •**PRESS PRINT**

THE NATURE OF VOICE WRITING

©Speaking Solutions 2001

People have the ability to carry on conversations and tell stories. Almost everyone can relate to a story and say something meaningful. And now they have the software to turn their speech into writing.

Voice-writing requires practice and lots of it. People adjust the pace of their writing to the efficiency of their input tools. In centuries past, writers would saddle their thoughts and slow them down to a walk when crafting paragraphs with pen and ink. Eventually, writers learned to type and entered their thoughts into typing machines at a trot, or even a gallop, to the rhythmic tapping of their fingers across the keyboard. By comparison, voice-writers produce copy at a run. Learning to think, compose, speak clearly, and edit at the speed of speech takes effort and rehearsal.

Inefficient keyboarding can retard the flow of ideas. It often causes writers, young writers in particular, to forget much of what they wish to communicate. Many potentially talented writers are intimidated or inhibited by their input tools. Inefficient typists, or those with poor penmanship, often shy away from the written craft. Poor scholars hesitate to write for fear that misspelled words will show them up.

But writing isn't spelling, typing, or penmanship. Writing is the artful communication of ideas in a written form. Speech recognition has made it possible for anyone who can think and speak clearly to write clearly as well. Inadequate spelling, erratic typing, or poor penmanship are no longer barriers to written expression. Writing can now become a process of thinking and expressing, supported by careful proof-reading and thoughtful editing.

These activities gave you practice dictating, editing and formatting reports using Text Edit. Additional exercises are included in the REINFORCEMENT ACTIVITIES section in the back of the book.

LESSON 11—Web Navigation, E-mails and Help

Dragon Dictate makes it possible to navigate the internet, conduct searches, and use e-mail programs with your voice. However, some web sites are more voice friendly than others. You can experiment and become familiar with what voice commands work best for you. The chart below shows some of the popular web navigation commands.

Say....	To....
OPEN or ACTIVATE (name of web browser)	Use Web Browser....Safari, Firefox, etc...
Do Web Search	Puts the cursor in the Search Field
Jump to Selection	Jumps to the selection in the current window
Move to Next (or Previous) Text Field	Moves the previous or next text field while in normal view
Jump Home	Takes yo to your home page
Scroll <up, down, left, right, to top or to bottom>	Scrolls the web pages
Create New Mail Message	Starts new e-mail message
Move to Beginning or End of message	Moves cursor to beginning or end of message

11.1 Enabling Web Commands

To enhance web browsing, there are 100 additional Web commands that can be enabled. To enable these commands:

- **Choose Preferences under the Dictate Menu on the Dragon Bar, choose the Command tab and make sure the Enable Website Commands AND Generate Email commands are checked and close the preferences window.**

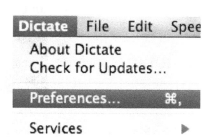
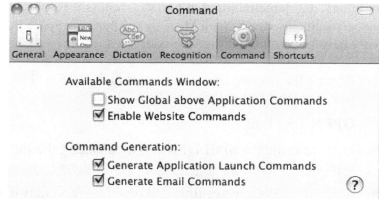

Say •**SHOW AVAILABLE COMMANDS**

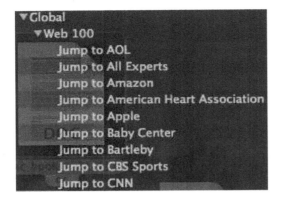

Notice a Web 100 list now appears under your global commands. This adds shortcuts for navigating to many popular websites.

11.2 Navigating the Internet

- To start a web browser such as Safari, you can either say "OPEN or ACTIVATE SAFARI" or name of web browser.

- The JUMP command will take you to many popular websites.

- You can say web addresses in the address bar just as you normally speak them. For example, to dictate "http://www.nuance.com/dragon", say "http www dot nuance dot com slash dragon"

- You can say the following web extensions by pronouncing them as words: com, gov, mil, net, org, and sys.

- Using the Spell Mode to spell in web addresses may be helpful for addresses that include unique letters and numbers. (See page 80 for more information on Spell Mode)

11.3 Using Spell Mode

In Spelling mode, you can both spell and give commands. Dragon Dictate will type individual letters, numbers, and punctuation that you say, unless it recognizes what you say as a command. No spaces are automatically inserted in Spell Mode so you must say Space Bar to insert any desired spaces. This can be very helpful when dictation web addresses.

- Be sure the Dictate Bar is frontmost and Say SWITCH TO SPELL MODE. Notice icon on status bar will show XYZ.

- **OPEN** Text Edit

- Practice using the SPELL MODE by dictating the following pretend web addresses one letter or symbol at a time: www.mpsaz123.org   upsne@gmail.com   pam.dilon@ed.sc.k_12.edu

- Spelling by voice takes time and practice. You may determine that it is easier to just key in unique addresses instead of using your voice. However, this is an individual choice.

- **QUIT** Text Edit, Press Don't SAVE

11.4 Practice Navigating

The following exercise gives you practice navigating the Internet and entering web addresses. (Let each page load before jumping to new page)

Say "DICTATION MODE" to make sure you are not still in Spell Mode
[OPEN Safari] (*wait for program to completely load*)
- Say • JUMP to USA Today
- Say • Scroll down (notice page will move down)
- Say • JUMP to Google, Say •Restaurants in Phoenix (text will appear in search box)
- Say • JUMP to Travelocity
- Say • JUMP to Utube
- Say • JUMP to Facebook
- Say • JUMP to Encylopedia Britannica

Visit two popular speech recognition sites:
- Use your mouse to click in the address bar
- Say • speaking no space solutions dot com (use your keyboard to press enter)
- Use your mouse to click in the address bar
- Say •http colon slash slash nuance dot com (use your keyboard to press enter)
- Use your mouse to select the address in the address bar
- Say SWITCH TO SPELL MODE
- Now Spell in the address speakingsolutions.com one letter at a time(use your keyboard to enter)
- Use your mouse to select the address in the address bar
- Now Spell in the address http://nuance.com
- •QUIT SAFARI or (Safari name of browser)

11.5 E-mail Commands

In addition to the Web 100 commands, we also enabled the Email commands feature:

- Say •SHOW AVAILABLE COMMANDS

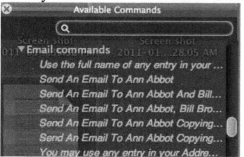

Notice Email commands also appear under your global commands. These are mainly commands for working with your own address book to send e-mails.

- Say •HIDE AVAILABLE COMMANDS

11.6   Creating E-mails

Using Dragon Dictate to create-mail messages follows the same dictation basics, correction techniques and formatting commands that you used to create other documents but also includes some built-in commands. Such as **Next Field, Previous Field, Send an Email To.** You can also include custom commands (MACROS).

Before following the steps to create an email, make sure you have created a custom command for your **teacher's email** and **your signature block**. See Lesson 8.10 Page 58 to review the steps for creating custom commands.

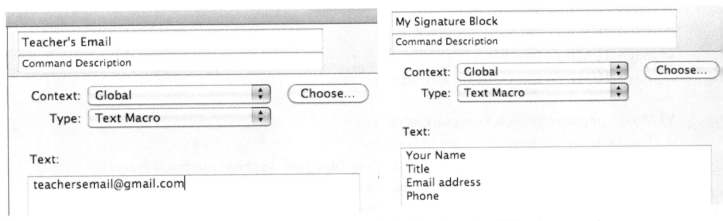

- Say: •**OPEN gmail** or (e-mail program of your choice) and try the following exercise:

- Click in the To: Field

- Say •**Teacher's email** (*this should enter the address of the custom command you just created.*)

- Say •**NEXT FIELD** (*you may need to repeat NEXT FIELD until cursor is in Subject field*)

- Say •Sample e-mail

- Say •**UPPERCASE** Sample e-mail

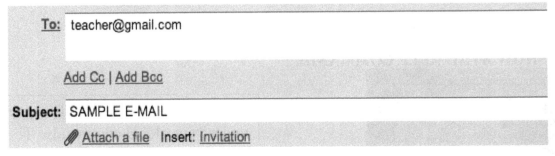

- Say •**NEXT FIELD** (*takes you to the body of the e-mail*)

- Dictate message:

  I am learning to use voice recognition software. This software allows me to talk and the computer will write what I say. Even though it may make some mistakes, it allows me to get my thoughts on the screen faster than when I type. I can always go back and make corrections either by voice or with my keyboard before I send a message. (NEW PARAGRAPH)

  It seems a little awkward to be talking to my computer. However, with some practice I think it will get much better at using Dragon Dictate and it all will help me to get my work done much faster. (NEW PARAGRAPH) MY SIGNATURE BLOCK

- Proofread and correct any errors.

- Click Send if you want to send the message

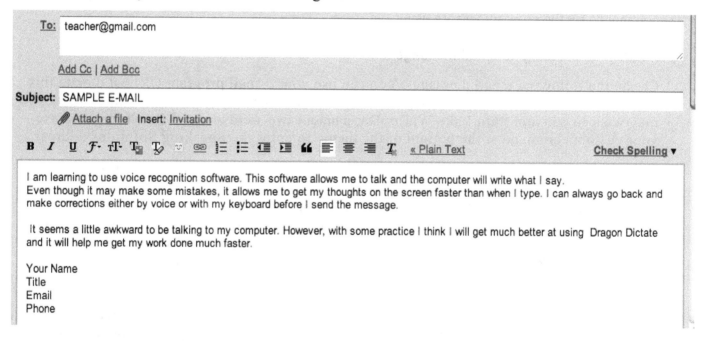

11.7 Learn More about Dragon Dictate

Dragon Dictate has several built-in features under the Dragon Dictate **Help** menu that can reinforce what you have learned or introduce you to more advance features.

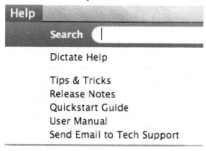

LESSON 12—Reinforcement Activities

You should now have a good basic understanding of how to use Dragon Dictate to dictate, edit, correct, train and format text. Remember, speech recognition is just an additional inputting tool. Depending on the project, sometimes the keyboard or mouse is the best tool for the task. However, speech recognition is generally the best tool for inputting large amounts of text quickly. Do not get discouraged if you are not proficient at speech recognition immediately. Learning a new skill takes time and requires practice.

The following activities will help you reinforce your speech recognition skills as you use a variety of programs to create a mixture of documents. You can use Dragon Dictate basic dictation techniques and commands with almost all other software programs. E-mail and word processing programs are the most popular because they are the most text intensive. However, voice-input can save time with many other applications. Remember, you can say "SHOW AVAILABLE COMMANDS" to see a list of commands for the program you are using.

Activity 1: Creating an email message

Create the following email message. You can use your e-mail program OR just dictate this message in Text Edit. Think about your attack strategies before you begin. For example, you may wish to add and train Lake WaConDa; a unique two-word location. Don't forget to use your custom command at the bottom of the memo to enter the Speaking Solutions address.

> **At 10:35 PM last evening, our business office in Lake WaConDa was hit by a tornado. Our tornado was one of seven to hit Union County in 24 hours. Businesses on both sides of our administrative center were damaged extensively. A building to the south was completely destroyed. Office supplies were found 200 feet away in a nearby field. A large tree branch was driven through the roof of the office complex next door. Fortunately, no employees were working late in the evening, and no one was injured.**
>
> **Luckily, there was only minimal damage to the Speaking Solutions warehouse which stores hundreds of thousands of dollars of inventory and supplies. The accounting office suffered water damage as a result of the rain that came with the tornado.**
>
> **All electrical power and online services to the Home Office will be off for another 72 hours as repairs are made. Please use ground mail services for all communications for the next few days. Send all correspondence to:**
>
> **Speaking Solutions Foundation**
> **2445 Lake Shore Drive**
> **Union, NE 68455**

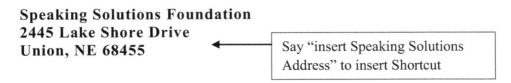

Say "insert Speaking Solutions Address" to insert Shortcut

- **Save document as**: Speaking Solutions e-mail

Activity 2: Creating Letters

Create the following letters using your voice. Think about your voice strategies. Dictate the city name, state name and zip code together. If you do so, Dragon Dictate will format the state codes properly and automatically. In other words, Nebraska will turn into NE. **Proofread, edit, save and print each letter when you are done.**

Letter 1

- **START NEW DOCMENT**

  INSERT TODAY'S DATE

  NEW PARAGRAPH
  NEW PARAGRAPH

  Dr. John Smith
  Jones Medical Center
  PO Box 52
  Big Springs, CO 50112 (*NEW PARAGRAPH*)

  Dear Dr. Smith (*NEW PARAGRAPH*)

  Dragon Dictate is the top-selling speech recognition software on the market today. We are sure you will be very pleased with the performance of your new software. Our local University Medical Center has been using the software successfully to reduce costs and to increase efficiency. Medical reports are now prepared in a fraction of the time. We are sure you will experience the same results in your medical center. *(NEW PARAGRAPH)*

  Please feel free to contact us if you have any questions or would like additional training for your medical team. *(NEW PARAGRAPH)*

  Sincerely
  NEW PARAGRAPH
  NEW PARAGRAPH

  Joe Brown
  President and CEO

- Proofread and correct all errors including correct capitalization.

- **SAVE DOCUMENT AS Letter 1**

LETTER 2

Insert your own information for the [ ] and use appropriate paragraph commands as in Letter 1

[Today's date]
Dear [FRIENDS NAME]

Many thanks for expressing an interest in my services. I realize there are numerous agents you might have chosen, so I greatly appreciate the opportunity to fulfill your insurance needs. I would consider it an honor and a privilege to work with you to achieve your business goals.

I am enclosing a packet of materials for you to review. Please note the highlighted text that addresses some of the concerns you shared.

Feel free to contact me anytime at [YOUF PHONE NUMBER], or visit my website at www.insurancefor you.com if you have questions or need more information.

Sincerely

[YOUR NAME]
Insurance Agent

Enclosure

Save Document As Letter 2 *(remember to say numeral 2)*

LETTER 3

[Today's date]
Dear [FRIENDS NAME}

One of the best things about life insurance is the way that it offers something that is very hard to find: peace of mind.

Life insurance enables you to live your life to the fullest without worrying about whether or not your loved ones will have the financial security they need in the future. You will know with certainty that they will be cared for and protected from any future financial difficulties that may arise in your absence.

Financial security for one's family is an immense gift indeed--and it is more attainable than most people realize. The key to acquiring this success and financial security is to establish an excellent life insurance policy that is perfectly attuned to the needs of your family.

You deserve the peace of mind that a good policy can afford, and so do your loved ones. Why not visit my Website www.lifeinsuranceforyou.com or give me a call today at [YOUR PHONE NUMBER] to discuss your options? There is no obligation, but you may find it is a perfect fit for your needs.

[Closing of your choice]

Save Document As Letter 3

Activity 3: Creating Reports

Think of all the reports you have had to write over the years and the time you spent handwriting or keying them. Now think about the time you can save using voice-input. Think about your voice strategies as you complete the following two reports.

Report 1

Remember you may want to add and train proper names such as Ediphone in this report. Say • COPYRIGHT SIGN for ©. Set your line spacing to **double**. *Remember, if you are in double space mode, use the • NEW LINE command instead of • NEW PARAGRAPH so only one blank line appears between paragraphs.*

Voice-Writing, Formatting and Editing
© Speaking Solutions Inc. 2010

 Dragon Dictate is a writer's tool. It allows composition without the physical constraints of a keyboard, mouse, pencil, or even a digital pen. Dragon allows your thoughts to verbally flow to the printed page.

 Voice-writing is nothing new. In the 1940s a tool called the Ediphone was used by executives to dictate correspondence. Ediphone users described their work as **voice-writing.** It's an apt term. Since then, companies like Dictaphone and Sony have made dictation devices for busy doctors, lawyers, executives, and others too preoccupied (or unqualified) to do their own typing.

 The popularity of voice-writing declined with the advent of the personal computer. An expectation grew during the 80s and 90s that everyone must learn to type their own written work. Typing became institutional. But the typing era is rapidly coming to a close as more efficient input tools are taught to a rapidly growing number of students, instructors, authors, and other professionals.

The Image of a Writer

 A century ago, the image of a writer was a lone individual sitting at a rugged wooden desk with a quill pen, parchment, and a half-empty ink bottle. (Picture Jefferson penning his memorable letters to John Adams from his desk at Monticello.) In the late 1800s, the imagery changed. With the creation of the typewriter by Christopher Latham Scholes in 1867, what it meant to be a writer was increasingly identified by the act of typing. The lone author plying his or her trade at a typewriter or keyboard became emblematic of what it meant to be a writer. Just as an idyllic Jeffersonian image was abandoned, this imagery will inevitably change.

 The depiction of writers at work today can portray entirely new stereotypes. Envision authors, journalists, or academics composing into mobile devices like iPhones or even smaller devices. They may be seen researching and voice-writing in the hallowed confines of a library — knowingly breaking the hushed silence. Writers can now combine digital pen input on smart screens with dictation. They may find themselves voice-writing while lounging at the beach, visiting a crime scene, investigating the site of a natural disaster, contemplating at a park, attending a press conference, or sitting alone at a local coffeehouse with their computer cradled like a clipboard.

 The thought of a writer wandering the city streets or the countryside voice-writing and dictating notes on smart screens paints a radically new image of a writer. New advances in speech recognition and computer technology are quickly making this image a reality.

Be sure the report is double- spaced, center title, proofread, edit and SAVE DOCUMENT AS Voice Writing Report.

Report 2

This was actually a newspaper article but can be formatted the same as a report. Glance through the report and add any unusual names of individuals or companies to your vocabulary before dictating. (See Lesson 8.1 page 48 to review adding words.) Remember, to dictate the retire report then use the "**READ THE DOCUMENT**" command to help you proofread. Correct each and every mistake using the **SELECT** and **SAY or CORRECT THIS** commands and apply all formatting features.

Keep this report in BLOCK format. Single space paragraphs and double-space between paragraphs. (Use NEW PARAGRAPH instead of NEW LINE to do this). Bold the title and the side headings.

WITH TECH SKILLS, YOU CAN CONQUER THE WORLD
(OR AT LEAST THE JOB MARKET) by Alex Foote
The Arizona Republic, Sunday, August 15, 2010

It's not always easy to master a new skill, especially a high-tech skill. But mastering technology skills can help you move forward in your career trajectory. People with cutting-edge high-tech skills always seem to find a job—even in the most hostile of job markets. That's because these individuals can do what others can't, and that makes them indispensable to employers.

How can you boost your technology skills to help you in the career search or job advancement? Here's what some career experts had to say:

Learn the Hottest Skills

All high-tech skills aren't created equal. You need skills that companies consider indispensable to their operations. For example, mobile-device skills are white hot. iPhones and their competitors have taken the high-tech world by storm, making the ability to develop applications, or apps, a priceless skill.

"People only exploit about 25 percent of the potential of the device," said Angela Fernando, tech column writer for *Communication World* magazine. "Just understanding how to maximize a piece of tech can help.*"

The Apple app store now has more than 185,000 apps, and companies are looking for people who can add more.

Master Search Engine Optimization

This is the practice of adjusting a website, through its coding or content, so that it appears as high as possible in the search engines results. The argument is that the higher a site is in their results, the more it will be clicked on.

Continue on next page

Start with a Book

When trying to learn high-tech skills, it can be easy to ignore the low-tech solutions. "If a person loves problem-solving and loves math, then picking up a book is a great way to get started," said Hamid Shojaee, CEO and founder of Axosoft, a Scottsdale-based software-development company.

The *Dummies* series is a great place for beginners with no experience to get their feet wet. You can start learning almost any programming language or any other technical skill this way.

Learn by Doing

Getting a high-tech job is more about your skills than formal training."Formal education isn't something that is ultra-important to me," said J. Belfore, Partner and Systems Director of New Angle Media in Phoenix. "It's more important to have an impressive portfolio of work."

Teaching yourself these skills is a viable option for someone who doesn't have the time or the money for school.

"All of your education can be done on the computer," Belfore said, "The tools necessary to write programs are essentially free." Try to develop a fully functional project from the ground up, based on an imaginary company or real customer, if possible. This should get you an impressive portfolio and maybe a little money at the same time.

Don't Abandon Your Current Skills.

While having new skills can help open doors, it's important to not abandon skills considered standards.

"High-tech companies... want people that have good problem solving and good creativity," said Bassam Matar, engineering professor at Chandler-Gilbert Community College.

Communication is--and always will be--key. After all, what is the point of creating a high-tech project if you can't get the word out?

Be sure you proofread, edit and SAVE DOCUMENT AS Activity 3 Report 2.

Activity 4: Formatting Text Using Cut, Copy and Paste Commands

In a new document, complete the following activity using cut, copy, paste, capitalization, bold, italics, center, underline and other formatting commands. To review formatting commands, go to Lesson 9.

1. Dictate the following sentences as written using the **NEW PARAGRAPH** command to separate the paragraphs. Use capitalization commands appropriately. Proofread and correct all misrecognized words before completing the exercises below.

   One of the holes is called Temptation Corner, and another one is called Valley of Danger. One of my favorite golf courses is CEDAR CREEK GOLF CLUB in Branson, Missouri. It was designed by John Adams, local golf professional.

   THE WORLD OF GOLF

   This course has some challenging holes – even for the experienced golfer. It is the most beautiful course in Missouri. You may want to take some extra balls with you if you play this course.

   Your First and Last Name

3. Use the cut, copy, center and paste voice commands to rearrange the above sentences into the paragraphs below. Format as directed below the paragraphs. Use your mouse to click the insertion points if you have trouble with the navigational commands. (Remember to use the **SELECT <beginning words> THROUGH <ending words>** to select an entire passage.

<u>THE WORLD OF GOLF</u>

One of my favorite golf courses is CEDAR CREEK GOLF CLUB in Branson, Missouri. It is the most beautiful course in Missouri. It was designed by John Adams, local golf professional.

This course has some challenging holes – even for the experienced golfer. One of the holes is called *Temptation Corner,* and another one is called *Valley of Danger.* You may want to take some extra balls with you if you play this course.

THE WORLD OF GOLF
By *Your Name*

4. Italicize Temptation Corner and Valley of Danger.

5. Center, Bold and Underline the title.

6. Save as: **Activity 4 world of golf**

Activity 5:   Taking Notes and Conducting Research by Voice

Taking notes is easy with speech recognition software. Instead of highlighting your text as you read or taking written notes, you can quickly dictate what you would highlight or write down. It is very easy to dictate exact passages and reference the page numbers for review later. Voice notes reinforce your reading comprehension and help you to create a summary of key points. In essence, your own quick study guides.

When conducting research, the Internet has become the research tool of choice for most people. Use your speech recognition software to help you navigate the web, organize your thoughts, take notes, keep track of your references and create a draft.

At first, you may feel a little uncomfortable talking to the computer, but after some practice, you'll find it easy and natural. The main thing is to speak naturally. Let the ideas flow from your brain to the screen. Speak your ideas as if you were answering a question for someone in person. This may help you overcome any awkward feelings that you have about talking to the computer.

Don't forget to turn off your microphone if you need some time to think or need to stop dictating for any reason. Remember the **RESUME WITH, INSERT BEFORE** and **INSERT AFTER** commands can be very helpful when composing with your voice. (See Page 64)

Taking notes for Report 2

Be sure you have completed the Activity 3 Report 2 document and have it printed for a hard copy reference. You will practice taking voice notes by answering questions about this article.

- First start a **New Document** and dictate "**These are my notes for Activity 3 Report 2 Article**" (NEW PRAGRAPH)

   *(Look at the printout of the article to answer the following **questions in complete sentences** using your voice)*

   1. What are the first two sentences under "Learn the hottest skills"?

   2. According to some career experts, what are the five ways you can boost your technology skills to help you in your career search or job advancement? (Hint: site headings in article, remember to use complete sentences).

   3. What quote in the article was stated by Hamid Shojaee, CEO and founder of Axosoft?

   4. What four things were quoted from J. Belfore, Partner and Systems Director of New Angle Media in Phoenix have the say?

   5. **SAVE DOCUMENT AS Notes for Report 2**

COMMAND QUICK SHEET

DICTATION COMMANDS	FUNCTION
Capitalize the Word[s] "text" [through/to "text"]	Capitalizes the instance of the word or phrase spoken that is closest to the insertion point.
Delete the Word[s] "text" [through/to "text"]	Deletes the instance of the word or phrase spoken that is closest to the insertion point.
Go to Beginning	Goes to the Beginning of the current document.
Go to End	Goes to the end of the current dictation session.
Insert After the Word[s] "text" [through/to "text"]	Moves the insertion point to just after the word or phrase you said.
Insert Before the Word[s] "text" [through/to "text"]	Moves the insertion point to just before the word or phrase you said.
Lowercase the Word[s] "text" [through/to "text"]	Makes all characters lowercase in the instance of the word or phrase spoken that is closest to the insertion point.
Move Backward [1-99] Words	Moves cursor back 1 to 99 words (Punctuation marks count as words)
Move Forward [1-99] Words	Moves cursor forward 1 to 99 words. (Punctuation marks count as words)
Move to Beginning of Document	Moves cursor to the beginning of the current document.
Move to End of Document	Moves cursor to the End of the current dictation session.
New Line	Presses the Return key once.
New Paragraph	Presses the Return key twice.
No Space	Types next word without a space before it.
Select the Word[s] "text" [through/to "text"]	Selects the instance of the word or phrase spoken that is closest to the insertion point.
Scratch That / Forget That	Deletes the last phrase you said, or to the left of where you insert the cursor.
Scratch Word / Forget Word	Deletes the last word you said, or to the left of where you insert the cursor.
Select All	Selects all text.
Train the Word[s] "text" [through/to "text"]	Selects, corrects the specified words in text, and trains them into profile as specified words are re-dictated.
Uppercase the Word[s] "text" [through/to "text"]	Makes all characters uppercase in the instance of the word or phrase spoken that is closest to the insertion point.

PHRASE TRAINING COMMANDS	FUNCTION
Choose "1" (or "2", etc.)	Chooses the specified item # in the Recognition window as the spoken and recognized phrase.
Pick "1" (or "2", etc.)	Corrects the selected text with the word or phrase that is item 1 (or 2, etc.) in the Recognition window.
Edit "1" (or "2", etc.)	Allows you to edit item 1 (or 2, etc.) in the Recognition Window.
Cancel Edit	Cancels all edits and restores all items in the Recognition window.
Press Play	Plays audio of most recent word or phrase dictated.
Hide Recognition Window	Closes the Recognition window.
Show Recognition Window	Opens the Recognition window.

DRAGON DICTATE WINDOW COMMANDS	FUNCTION
Show Status Window	Shows the Status window for Dragon Dictate.
Hide Status Window	Hides the Status window for Dragon Dictate.
Show Available Commands Window	Shows the Available Commands window for Dragon Dictate.
Hide Available Commands Window	Hides the Available Commands window for Dragon Dictate.

Bring Dictate to the Front	Makes Dictate the frontmost application.
Show Recognition Window	Opens the Recognition window.
Hide Recognition Window	Closes the Recognition window.

CAPITALIZATION COMMANDS	FUNCTION
Caps On	Turns on capitalizing the first letter of every word.
Caps Off	Turns off capitalizing the first letter of every word.
Cap	Capitalizes the next word spoken.
All Caps	Types the next word spoken in CAPS.
All Caps On	Makes every word CAPS.
All Caps Off	Returns capitalization to normal.
No Caps	Makes the next word spoken lower case.
No Caps On	Makes the following text lowercase until turned off.
No Caps Off	Returns capitalization to normal.
Capitalize the Word[s] "text" [through/to "text"]	Capitalizes the identified word or phrase spoken that is closest to the insertion point.

NO SPACE COMMANDS	FUNCTION
No Space On	Turns the No Space mode on, so there is no space between words.
No Space Off	Turns the No Space mode off
No Space	Types the next word

BUTTON/KEYBOARD COMMANDS	FUNCTION
Press Cancel	Press the Cancel Button.
Press Don't Save	Press the Don't Save Button.
Press OK	Press the OK Button.
Cancel This Operation	Cancels the current operation.
Save This Document	Mimics a Command-S keypress; Saves frontmost document in most apps.

MENU COMMANDS	FUNCTION
File New	Selects the New menu item on the File Menu.
File Open	Selects the Open menu item on the File Menu.
File Close	Selects the Close menu item on the File Menu.
Undo Last Action	Undoes the last action. Same as using keyboard, so Scratch That or Undo Dictation are preferred.
Redo Last Action	Redo last action reverses the effect of the "Undo Last Action" command.
About this Application	Displays information about the frontmost application.
Access Find Window	Opens the Find window.
Access Force Quit Window	Opens the Force Quit window.
Show Date and Time	Displays a dialog box with the date and time stamp.

APPLICATION LAUNCH/QUIT COMMANDS	FUNCTION
Activate [Application Name]	Activates (Opens/Launches) the named application.
Open [Application Name]	Opens (Activates/Launches) the named application.
Launch [Application Name]	Launches (Opens/Activates) the named application.
Quit [Application Name]	Quits (Kills) the named application.
Kill [Application Name]	Kills (Quits) the named application.

CHAT COMMANDS	FUNCTION
Send Message	Sends the current message.
Smiley Face	:-)
Frowny Face	:-(
Winky Face	;-)

SPELLING MODE - EXAMPLES	FUNCTION
a b c	abc
1 2 3 EXCLAMATION POINT	123!
a SPACEBAR b SPACEBAR c	a b c
a b CAP c	abC
a b c SCRATCH THAT	ab
a b c MOVE BACKWARD 1 CHARACTER d	abdc

TEXT EDITING COMMANDS	FUNCTION
Cache Document	Prepares pasted text from other applications for editing by dictation.
Cache Selection	Prepares the selected text for navigation by voice or editing by dictation.
Copy Selection	Copies the selected text.
Cut Selection	Cuts the selected text.
Next Field	Performs the Purge Cache command, then tabs to next field in current application.
No Leading Space	Only for words already dictated -- All spaces are removed before the word immediately after the cursor or left edge of the selection.
Paste From Clipboard	Pastes text from clipboard.
Previous Field	Performs the Purge Cache command, then tabs to previous field in current application.
Purge Cache	Commits dictated text to an existing document.
Redo Last Action	Tells active application to perform most recent action again.
Undo Last Action	Tells active application to undo most recent action. Equal to Cmd-Z keyboard shortcut in many applications.
Select All	Selects all text.

KEY COMMANDS	FUNCTION
Press The Key [keyname]	Enters the keyname as though the key had been pressed on the keyboard. Keynames are alphabet keys, numbers, function key F1 - F20, or other named keys
Press The Key Combo [modifiers][keyname]	Enters the modifier keys, plus the keyname, as though they had been pressed on the keyboard. Modifiers are Control, Shift, Command, Option, Function and Capslock. Keynames are alphabet keys, numbers, function key F1 - F20, or other named keys.

Terms of Use

Please read before accessing this information, either in print, online, or on CD.

This training manual contains instructional materials, documentation and other information related to products and services of Speaking Solutions Incorporated, a Nebraska-based corporation. (Also referred to as "SpeakingSolutions.com" or "Speaking Solutions"). This information is provided as a courtesy to customers of Speaking Solutions, Incorporated and those who have been trained by Speaking Solutions Incorporated consultants or trainers. By accessing or using any information contained herein, you agree to be bound by the terms and conditions described in these Terms of Use.

Copyright Notice

Unless otherwise marked, these training materials, documentation, and other materials contained at the www.speakingsolutions.com website or on training CDs are owned and copyrighted by Speaking Solutions, Incorporated. Copyright © 1999 – 2013 Speaking Solutions, Incorporated, 2445 Lake Shore Drive, Lake WaConDa, Union, NE 68455. All rights reserved.

Other Intellectual Property Rights

Speaking Solutions, Incorporated, Speaking Solutions and SpeakingSolutions.com, and other names of Speaking Solutions products, product features, and services are the property of Speaking Solutions, Incorporated in the United States and other countries. Speaking Solutions, Incorporated also uses the following trademarks that are not currently registered with the USPTO. Some of these trademarks are the subject of trademark applications and may become registered in the future: SpeakingSolutions.Com, Speaking Solutions, Nifty 50, Nifty 58, Nifty 59 and Speech Recognition Applications: The Basics and Beyond.

Other product and company names mentioned in this material, or on the web site, on CD or other printed materials are the trademarks of their respective owners. Nothing contained in these Terms of Use shall be construed as conferring by implication, estoppel, or any other legal theory, a license or right to any patent, trademark, copyright, or other intellectual property right, except those expressly provided herein. The products, processes, software, and other technology described may be the subject of other intellectual property rights owned by Speaking Solutions, Incorporated or by third parties.

Disclaimer

NO WARRANTIES: THE TRAINING MATERIALS PROVIDED IN PRINT AND AT THE WEBSITE OR DISTRIBUTED ON CD IS "AS IS" WITHOUT ANY EXPRESS OR IMPLIED WARRANTY OF ANY KIND INCLUDING WARRANTIES OF MERCHANTABILITY, NONINFRINGEMENT OF INTELLECTUAL PROPERTY, OR FITNESS FOR ANY PARTICULAR PURPOSE. IN NO EVENT SHALL SPEAKING SOLUTIONS INCORPORATED BE LIABLE FOR ANY DAMAGES WHATSOEVER (INCLUDING, WITHOUT LIMITATION, DAMAGES FOR LOSS OF PROFITS, BUSINESS INTERRUPTION, OR LOSS OF INFORMATION) ARISING OUT OF THE USE OF THE CONTENT PROVIDED, EVEN IF SPEAKING SOLUTIONS INCORPORATED HAS BEEN ADVISED OF THE POSSIBILITY OF SUCH DAMAGES BECAUSE SOME JURISDICTIONS PROHIBIT THE EXCLUSION OR LIMITATION OF LIABILITY FOR CONSEQUENTIAL OR INCIDENTAL DAMAGES.

SPEAKING SOLUTIONS, INCORPORATED FURTHER DOES NOT WARRANT THE ACCURACY OR COMPLETENESS OF THE INFORMATION,TRAINING, INSTRUCTION, TEXT, GRAPHICS, LINKS OR OTHER ITEMS CONTAINED WITHIN THE WEBSITE, CD, OR PRINTED COPY. SPEAKING SOLUTIONS, INCORPORATED MAY MAKE CHANGES TO THESE MATERIALS, OR TO THE PRODUCTS DESCRIBED THEREIN, AT ANY TIME WITHOUT NOTICE. SPEAKING SOLUTIONS, INCORPORATED MAKES NO COMMITMENT TO UPDATE THIS INFORMATION.

INDEX

www.ingramcontent.com/pod-product-compliance
Lightning Source LLC
Chambersburg PA
CBHW060453060326
40689CB00020B/4519